uplake

uplake

RESTLESS ESSAYS
OF COMING AND GOING

Ana Maria Spagna

UNIVERSITY OF WASHINGTON PRESS
Seattle

Uplake was published with the support of the Northwest Writers Fund, which promotes the work of some of the region's most talented nonfiction writers and was established through generous gifts from Linda and Peter Capell, Janet and John Creighton, Ruth and Alvin Eller, Michael J. Repass, and other donors.

Printed and bound in the United States of America

Design by Katrina Noble
Cover photograph by Michal Janek on Unsplash
Composed in Cassia, typeface designed by Dieter Hofrichter
22   21   20   19   18   5   4   3   2   1

UNIVERSITY OF WASHINGTON PRESS
www.washington.edu/uwpress

CATALOGING-IN-PUBLICATION DATA IS ON FILE
WITH THE LIBRARY OF CONGRESS.

ISBN 978-0-295-74322-6 (PBK), ISBN 978-0-295-74323-3 (EBOOK)

If I could do just one near-perfect thing I'd be happy.

They'd write it on my grave, or when
they scatter my ashes.

On second thought I'd rather hang about and
be there with my best friend

If she wants me.

—BELLE & SEBASTIAN

• ——————————————— •

For Laurie
For being there

CONTENTS

uplake

PROLOGUE

Here's a story line. A boy grows up in an idyllic place, a small rural place, the plains of Nebraska, say, or small-town North Carolina. What happens next? He moves away. His new perspective may cause him to grow nostalgic like Jim Burden in *My Ántonia* or world-weary like George Webber in *You Can't Go Home Again*, but when he returns—sophisticated, citified, wizened—he sees the place anew. Here's another. A woman drops everything to go into the wild, to take a long hike and test her mettle, to confront grief or addiction or depression. What happens next? She moves back to the city, rejuvenated and renewed, and marries and has a family and lives happily ever after. It's the archetypal journey, the stuff of Carl Jung, Joseph Campbell, Northrop Frye, as familiar to us—to our collective unconscious, they say—as a three-chord rock song or a five-act play. We anticipate the resolution, the triumphant return, the chorus after the bridge.

Here's another story. A girl grows up in sun-washed suburbs and moves to the woods, not just any woods but the most distant and remote she can find, a place where glaciers

3

still carve and rivers still sculpt and the local black bear population outnumbers the humans. Then she stays.

That's not a story. That's stasis. Or maybe it's commitment.

There's a moment at every dinner party when the dreaded questions arise. You begin to sweat because you're about to be introduced as a writer and you're going to have to explain if you've ever been published (you have) and if they've heard of your books (they haven't), or you'll be introduced to people who don't yet know you're gay and you'll either have to do some fancy pronoun footwork or make a big pronouncement. Those are tough questions, but not as tough, anymore, as when people ask where I live. My home is beautiful. Check that, it's way past beautiful; it's pristine, spectacular, majestic, maybe even sublime.

You're so lucky to live there, people say.

I am lucky. But I am also restless. It's easy to get feeling stuck, oppressed, not just by the close valley walls or the long sunless days of winter or even the lack of a grocery store or a library or the chance, ever, for anonymity, but by the stuckness itself. So I fly away. I drive long highway miles. I fantasize about moving. And though my case may be extreme, I suspect I'm not alone in this.

The problem with the word "commitment" is that it sounds so much like work or at least like a conscious decision. What about wonder? The kind that strikes you broadside when you see the first spawning Kokanee shimmering under the surface or the first yellow larch on a ridgetop backlit by sunrise. There's wonder in the smell of a campfire across the lake; the rolling carpet rump of a bear spooked on a trail run; the half-drunk swoop of pileated woodpeckers; in the way rock spire shadows stretch across a snowy bowl and ice chunks form on the river like floating mirrors, tinkling; and dogwood flowers appear in spring, white and showy, then turn papery and drop. There's wonder, too, in the sadness when the last maple leaf dangles on a limb and the last seasonal neighbors, bags packed, wait for the ferry. There's wonder even in the sameness, the plotlines that recur predictable as sitcoms or soap operas—wildlife encounters and wild exuberant parties—and those that escalate in the age of climate change: fires and floods, big snows and hot summers.

Meanwhile, each morning I drink coffee and pull on my running shoes. Usually I don't want to go. I tell myself I can skip this one day. It's too cold or too hot or too wet or too dusty. I have work to do. But this is the only meditation practice I have, the dregs of the prayers I was taught as a child. Name what you see. Offer gratitude. Not every story is a circle. Sometimes it's just one foot in front of the other.

Slow Connection

THIS MORNING, LIKE MOST MORNINGS, I SIT AT MY DESK in Stehekin gazing out my window and cursing. Make no mistake, there's nothing wrong with the view: a lovely mixed-species forest—fir, maple, cottonwood, dogwood, cedar—and McGregor Mountain dramatically shadowed with early morning light. The problem is my Internet connection. It used to be fast when we first got hooked up, back when satellite trumped dial-up, then came DSL, then wireless, and websites got snazzier, and our speedy satellite fell behind like a tricycler trying to keep up with the big kids. Some solutions might work: pay for more bandwidth, cut some trees, buy yet another new laptop. Then there's the obvious: shut it off and go outside! I know I should. Instead I sit watching the proverbial pot, drumming my fingers (Come on! Come on!) and considering what's become of me.

Twenty-five years ago, a friend, a man I respected for his kindness, his devotion to his own mountain valley—the Skagit, on the rainy west side of the North Cascades—and its inhabitants, and especially, his willingness to fix my run-down Corolla for cheap, approached me at a memorial service for a mutual friend like an evangelist. His voice dropped with sincerity, his eyes met mine. The answer, he explained, was obvious. The answer to what? I wondered.

He leaned closer.

"The Information Superhighway," he said.

I was annoyed. Super annoyed. Maybe I should have seen some humor in the ridiculous Jetson-esque name or the irony of a hippie mechanic espousing it. The Information Superhighway? Who had heard of such a thing?

Well, I had. That was the problem. I'd read about so-called modem cowboys snatching up land in the Mountain West with no need to commute, citifying things, sending property taxes skyrocketing. I didn't know what a modem was, exactly, but I knew all about citification since I'd grown up in the vast sprawling outer edges of Los Angeles, and I'd come to the North Cascades to escape it.

I was hardly the first. My mechanic friend had arrived in the Skagit a generation before me with a slew of young back-to-the-landers who shirked the city to huddle under

Visqueen and dance around slash piles, to start tree-planting co-ops and organic farms. In the early nineties, just out of college, I aspired to that kind of life even as I felt it dying all around me. Our mutual friend, a trail worker in his forties—a man so handsome I couldn't look him in the eye without my knees going weak—had died of complications related to AIDS, though no one spoke of it yet as such. A photo display at the memorial service captured him in the early heady days: building soil for the flower beds he'd later tend to extravagance, camping in dense old-growth forests that were long since gone. I was depressed. I'd arrived too late. If I needed any more evidence than clear-cuts or AIDS, now I had the Information Superhighway charging toward me.

I didn't have any idea what to say to my friend, but just as I tried to figure it out, he changed tack.

"When are you two going to move in for real?"

He meant my partner, Laurie, and me. We'd been living for a couple of years in a small cedar cabin overlooking the river in Rockport. Now, he told me, there might be an opening in the land co-op he and his friends started way back when.

"We could use some new blood up here," he said.

The invitation represented an honor, I knew, a gesture of generosity, of camaraderie, but I knew, even then, that I couldn't move to the Skagit permanently for a bunch of reasons. The weather was too drippy, the woods too dark, the hippie legacy heavy as moss clinging carpet-thick to cedar bark. Dylan whined on a turntable, and suddenly I felt claustrophobic.

"I haven't yet grown my web feet," I said.

A lame answer. He'd been reaching out, and I'd turned to tourist cliché.

Disconnect.

The room looked different. Not just the mildew in the community hall, built to mimic a Native American long-house, or the vinyl moan of *Blood on the Tracks*. My friends were in their forties. Their sinewy bodies had worn knobby and off-kilter from too much physical labor, their relationships had cracked under stress. What in the city might have seemed like everyday middle-aged crises, out here scared me sick. They'd been so idealistic, they'd worked so hard, and still their connection to this bucolic place seemed tenuous. For many of them, including the bereaved partner of the handsome trail worker, the bigger town, Bellingham, beckoned.

I raced home to the cabin, switched on Lyle Lovett, and dreamed of riding a pony on a boat in the ocean, somewhere far away.

Laurie and I did eventually settle, not in the Skagit but thirty miles east, over the Cascade Crest, in Stehekin—a word that means "the way through," a place named for a narrow pass at the head of the valley that Native people used for trade—where the sun shone more often and precipitation came as snow rather than rain. I spent my days working on trails for the National Park Service, walking by creeks too loud to hear yourself think and past views so stunning words won't ever do: translucent-blue glaciers and columbine-red meadows and a thousand peaks staggering out toward the horizon like jagged incisors, like sails on the wind, while Laurie worked in a picturesque historic orchard. In our off time from work, we worked more. We milled lumber to build our own cabin and screened soil for a garden and mortared rocks, one by one, to the concrete foundation of the house. Life was good.

And over time it grew old. One evening during a late season campout, I left my crew and hiked three miles at dusk just to sleep in my own bed and woke at dawn to hightail it back to work in the woods. In that jinglejangle morning light, watching the early bustle of folks heading to work—idling to chat through pickup truck windows, waving with a coffee cup from a bicycle—I felt something in me break. I wasn't sure I could keep doing trail work. I wasn't sure I wanted to. I'd later say the problem was my body—knobby, yes, off-kilter, sure—but really, my body, at thirty-eight, was fine, just fine, maybe not as strong as it once was, but a whole lot tougher. The problem wasn't even that I felt lonely or bored or plain tired, though sometimes I did. The problem was that I felt disconnected from almost everything in the whole wide world save my small crew and the dirt I slept on.

Right around that time, the Superhighway came charging in. Up until that point, high ridges, Wilderness regulation, and plain Luddite tradition had kept roads and even telephones out of Stehekin. Now satellite dishes sprouted like mushrooms on one cabin then the next. Laurie and I were slow to connect, among the very last in the valley to cave, figuring you're either part of the problem or part of the solution. But after that morning when trails lost their luster, I signed us up. Just like that. Here it was: the answer! A hunk of plastic the size of a saucer sled perched on a galvanized post designed to send a signal to a hunk of metal in the sky and back down. At least as ridiculous as a pony on a boat. And just as liberating.

No one needs me to recount the riches of the Internet, twenty years late, like the sweet baubles gleaned in trade. Email, of course (remember, we had no phone), but so much more: political screeds, music podcasts, Latin names for plants, recipes for Swiss chard, statistics on black bear populations. Our world could not have changed more if we'd moved to Uzbekistan. What was the Internet the answer to? Restlessness. Ignorance. Middle age. Everything.

When I was a kid outside Los Angeles, the "freeway capital of the world," we didn't use the freeways that much. Not daily, at least. Surface streets got us kids to school and my parents to work. We used the 91 freeway to get away, to go to Disneyland or Angels games or to the beach, forty-five miles on three freeways, six lanes each way, past Corona surrounded by dry hills waiting to burn, through Anaheim Hills, then past the red-tiled houses and gated golf courses and Mercedes Benzes until the ocean showed on the horizon like a thick swatch of oil paint, bluer than blue, the wide expanse of mystery and seduction. That's exactly how the Internet felt at first.

Suddenly I lived not in one small community but several. I wrote for editors online, taught classes online, and corresponded with friends I'd never met in person. I could connect anytime from my solitary desk in Stehekin, from beside my mother's hospital bed in California, from musty motel rooms on the road. From anywhere to anywhere. The friendships grew like all good connections, slowly over time. As did the amount of time I spent on my ass.

What I didn't understand in those discussions of modem cowboys was that the problem wasn't just that the newcomers would raise property taxes or that they wouldn't contribute to the local economy or even—the reason that most miffed me at the time—that they wouldn't earn their keep the old-fashioned way, out in the rain with socks drying by the campfire and grommets rusting on their tarps. It was that they'd both be there and not be there, like the residents of a bedroom community. Their real lives would be somewhere else.

Turns out the problem with the Information Superhighway isn't the people who come speeding into the woods but the ones like me who seep slowly away. Kind of like Cascade Pass, the way through. Surely the trade route made life richer, but it came with a price. I imagine ancient Stehekinites worried about strangers who might arrive over the pass, take an approving look around, and elbow in to stay, but I'll bet they also worried about the ones, especially the young ones, who hoofed it out and never returned. In some ways, as soon as I hung up my work gloves, cut my jeans into rags, and entered a world in pixels on a screen, I began to lose my shared-dirt connections here at home. It's not as if I didn't know that from the get-go.

Tonight on the radio—streaming via the Internet from Seattle twenty-four thousand miles into space and back down—reporters discussed the interstate freeway system, how poor communities disproportionately lost their homes and businesses during construction and afterward suffered noise and pollution and increased property taxes. I looked up the permitting documents to wade through the justifications, which were familiar as dirt: more growth, more economic prosperity. City officials and federal highway planners figured freeways to be the answer. The answer to what? To everything! Connecting cities and parts of cities, to be sure, but also to urban blight. Another three clicks of a mouse and I find the truth, also familiar, dirtier yet: urban planners across the country used freeway construction to eliminate perceived problems, to fracture black communities and displace families. As I sit and wait for the page to load so I can read more, I notice the option at the bottom right-hand corner of the page "Loading standard view, Load basic HTML (for slow connections)." That gets me thinking about the standard view. If the standard view of interstates—the one I learned in school and never questioned until now—was all Eisenhower triumph and patriotic wonder, what's the standard view of the Internet? What does it fracture? Who does it displace? How long will it take us to figure that out?

The cursor blinks and stalls, the tiny icon circles round and round—buffering, buffering (to buffer: to lessen the shock of, to cushion or protect)—and my impatience morphs back into selfishness. My complaints include these: I can't watch YouTube or talk on Skype. I can download photos but not upload them. I can stream radio but not in high-quality sound. When it rains, I lose my connection or it slows to a crawl, so it might take twenty seconds for an email to send, a full minute with an attachment. If someday I get high-speed Internet, I sometimes think I'll have more time for other things. But I suspect I'll just have more time for high-speed Internet. That's how addiction works, isn't it? You'll drink what you have. You'll need more to get high. And it's not just personal; it's everybody needing it at once. (So many of us sitting on our asses!) The truth about those California freeways I knew as a kid is that they were not fast moving at all but clogged bumper to bumper the entire way to the beach and home, six lanes either way. Other people may remember even older routes—the back roads and city streets of yesteryear—but it's hard for me to believe they were any slower than the unmoving 91 on a glary afternoon. Anymore, if I lived in Southern California, I don't think I'd bother going to the beach. I'd just stay home.

Some of those old hippies I knew and loved still live in the Skagit Valley. They stayed put on that narrow two-lane highway, in those drippy long winters and the doghair forests, and I admire them for that. Just as I admire my sister for staying in the city where we grew up, teaching sixth graders whose parents have, often as not, arrived in Southern California from elsewhere only to find assimilation to be slow at best. I have always had a desperate admiration for those who lay claim and sit steady. I aspire to it, I *believe* in it, and for many years now I've worked at it, even as the allure of distant places—more interesting, more diverse, more lively—dogs me. Maybe the Internet will help change that, for me and for people in rural remote places everywhere. Maybe we can have our cake and eat it too: stay put and sally forth.

Or maybe I should chuck it.

Here's the truth: I want the Internet. I do not think that giving it up would improve my life or my commitment to my neighbors or to this lovely place. I used to wear a Walkman in the woods in the pre-iPod days—half a dozen cassettes hogged a precious six-inch square of my weeklong pack—and I'd face hard scorn from other hikers on the trail. Can't you do without it? the scorners seemed to think. Even for a short time? I could, but I chose not to. Call it distraction or inspiration. I knew that I walked faster, worked harder, thought clearer, felt happier with my Walkman on. So why take it off? Ditto for the Internet. My life is richer for it. But sometimes (right now?) I need to shut the damned thing off and go outside.

More Than Noise

A DISTANT CHAINSAW SOUNDS LIKE A WOMAN SCREAMING for help, but as you move closer, it sounds more like a full-throated tenor. To a bystander, a chainsaw stinks like gas fumes, but to the operator, it smells like pungent wood: cedar or pine or cottonwood or fir. The weight of a saw in your hands—a familiar saw, say, a Stihl 026—feels like a toddler, and you hold it like a toddler too—firm but not tight, cautious and attentive and sometimes playful, always in motion—you must triangulate your own body movement with that of the power head and the tree you will cut. The generic image of the chainsaw is big and loud and danger-ous, a tool for destruction. But up close it's more intimate.

For much of my adult life, I ran a chainsaw daily, clearing downed trees from hiking trails and building bridges and shelters and picnic tables. Sometimes, but not always, I was the only woman on the crew. A woman running a chainsaw might surprise hikers or strangers at picnic-table dinner parties who only associate women and chainsaws with the sexy models in early Stihl catalogs—women straddling saws, women on swings with saws. But after fifteen years, my gender made little difference. I loved my job, and I did it well. I miss it—not just the satisfaction of so-called honest work or the astonishing alpine beauty or the achy buzz of being hyper-fit—but the saw itself.

That sound. The scream, the song, yes, or often a high-pitched whine—louder, harsher, teeth gnashingly so—dulled by my yellow foam earplugs to a jet-plane roar. Then an octave drop. The sound of the saw bogging down, losing power, the air filter or the muffler clogged, or more likely the tension in the log shifting, threatening to pinch your bar. Or worse. Once a friend sawed a log that had fallen across the trail from the downhill side—never saw from the downhill side—and the cut round rolled toward her. She hit the ground flat and fast, and the log bounced right over. Luckily she wore a hard hat. I never did. No hard hat, no safety glasses, no chaps. What was I thinking? Three people I know cut into their own legs. Ragged flesh, lots of blood, stitches, a chip of bone.

In all those years, I never got injured. Unless you count the walnut-sized bulge along my spine at the bra line, not from running the saw but from carrying it on one shoulder—the right, always the right—for hours every day, for miles, with the chain brake on, the steel teeth in my leather-gloved hand. I know. I know. I should have switched shoulders, and I should've used a plastic sheath or wrapped protective chaps around the bar, but the chaps were bulky and the sheath would slip, and I felt more in control holding the teeth in my glove, even if they sat there on my shoulder, day after day, inches from my carotid artery. Once I watched a friend saw barefoot—balanced on a log across a creek. Once I stood sock-footed on a tall friend's shoulders to cut a high limb. We took crazy risks and laughed about them later, but we never bragged about them, ever. I'm not bragging now but trying to remember the way you try to remember a friend who's left or died, a friend you didn't know you cared about so much.

We felled live trees, but rarely. Usually the trees we bucked had already fallen; they were just in the way. Sometimes the logs were suspended, wedged between standing trees, and the resulting tension could cause a log to spring back or drop down or even stand straight up, Lazarus-like, if the weight of the dirt clinging to the roots was enough to pull it upright. (Sometimes weekend volunteers would tell stories of this happening as if it were rare, magical, shocking. We'd never correct them. We'd never say: that happens all the time. Better, always, to let stand a belief in a marvelous phenomenon than to insist it's mundane.) Fresh-cut chips—white, yellow, and orange—lay in the dirt long past when the tree was gone, like piles of hamster bedding. I could walk a trail on my days off and tell how recently it'd been worked by the brightness of those chips on the ground.

The guys always wanted to run the 044—the bigger, heavier saw that cuts faster and burned through gas like a hummingbird through sugar water. The guys liked the power. They liked the fact that they did not have to bend so far to cut a log lying on the ground. They did not mind schlepping the extra weight, but I did. The 026 was my size (10.7-pound power head, 2.97-cubic-inch displacement, 20-inch bar, three-eighth-inch pitch chain). After a while, after a few years and a few hundred trees, the 026 began to feel like an appendage.

The only machines I've known as well as chainsaws are cars and computers. I can fix neither of those to save my life, but I could repair the 026. I could change the filters, air or fuel; replace a sprocket, careful not to lose the C-clip when releasing it with needle-nose pliers; replace a pull cord or muffler. I could adjust a carburetor. And I could sharpen. I sharpened the chain many times a day at a workbench or, more often, on my knees in the dirt counting the strokes—you must file each tooth the same number of times or, well, you are screwed—in the sun, in the bugs, while the crew talked, or actually didn't talk. They knew better than to talk or I'd lose count. We used the saws so hard and sharpened the chains so often that in a month a tooth the length of a pencil eraser could be reduced to a fingernail snip. If you let it get to that, the tooth will break. You have to know when to give up on a chain.

Long before I ever ran a chainsaw, I used a crosscut saw. The Forest Service, unlike the Park Service, allows nothing motorized, nothing mechanized, in federally designated Wilderness. A crosscut requires more patience and care; if you get the saw stuck, you'll have to chop it out with an axe. The cuts take longer, so you make fewer of them and, as a result, the rounds you cut are bigger, so you want to think about where they'll drop and roll. There's a hint of historic reenactment—two sawyers on either side of a log taking turns pulling; you may as well wear a pair of suspenders—and there's commitment to an ideal, a rejection of the screaming whining roar of modernity, especially modernity in the woods. But even those who love the crosscut most, even those who use it best, will admit the crosscut is nonsense. If you want to get work done, you need a chainsaw.

Here's how you start: You pull until you feel the resistance and then drop the saw fast to break the compression. Sometimes, when the saw won't start, on a hot day there might be vapor lock or too much soot on the muffler. Or you might've flooded it. So you wait and then pull some more. Back when I was learning, a friend gave me a used copy of *Barnacle Parp's Chainsaw Guide* by Walter Hall, copyright 1977, that covered the basics of operation and maintenance. Barnacle Parp was an alter ego for the author, a faux wise woodsman, and the campiness put me off. I flipped through the ragged-cover copy as necessary, usually only when something was broken. Mostly I sawed. I bloodied my fingers learning to start, and I never looked back.

The chainsaw has wreaked havoc, undeniably, in Pacific Northwest forests even more than in Texas massacre films. But it's not so simple, not all one thing. On trail crew, we built things too: benches and bridges and shelters that would last decades. We'd scribe the logs, then notch them—make parallel cuts and chip the chunks out with an axe—and then run the saw across the grain quickly at half throttle, working it like a sander. When the notch was deep and smooth as a salad bowl, you could start the next one. That way you could fit the logs together snug and right as bodies entwined in sleep to make something sturdy and functional, sometimes beautiful. Everyday acts of creation to balance the destruction.

Part of me knows I'll never be that close to the chainsaw again, inside the roar, right inside of it, where the worst we humans do meets the best we do, and one wrongly timed move can hurt you so badly, or hurt others. Hell, a car can do the same. Ditto a ballot or a dollar or a series of mouse clicks all in a row. The chainsaw may be louder and sharper, but at least you know what you're up against. You know what you're capable of, what you're responsible for, and anyway, we all know the truth: it's not, in the end, what tool you use but how you use it.

Once, outside a cabin, I spur-climbed a Doug fir and hung from my lanyard, limbing the tree with a very small saw while, without my knowledge, a woman inside the cabin was getting a massage. Bad timing. Later, the massage therapist, a friend, told me her client did not mind, that she'd said she could hear no aggression in the noise. The client could not have known that a woman was at work, not a man, but I wondered, was that the difference? God knows testosterone plus a chainsaw sometimes equals aggression. (Ditto for the car, ballot, and dollar, you might say.) But it's not all gender. Even if you've never run a saw, you can hear when someone is forcing the issue, fighting the wood, revving past the time for an undercut. The grain is tightening, and the sawyer doesn't know enough or is not paying enough attention to pull out the bar and saw upward to meet the downward cut. It's rare to cut only one direction and make it work.

A decade ago, I decided to put down the chainsaw. It would be easy to say I'd had it, that I wanted to live a life less dirty, less loud, less smelly. That is not true. Nor was it my biological clock ticking, though that is the reason many women stop. In my early twenties, I'd hitched myself to Laurie, and we'd long since decided our seasonal lifestyles and our lousy paychecks and our conservative rural town would not make it easy to raise children. I was tired and restless, eager to try a new path, a more conventional path in a way: writing and teaching. But I never regretted the hard labor I did because of the rich life it provided.

The chainsaw allowed Laurie and me to make men's wages, which outpace those for women's work in our rural town by at least threefold. The chainsaw gave us the confidence to build a house and to use other tools. By the time our house was complete, Laurie kept a bandsaw in the living room. She used it to make cabinet handles from apple prunings and to cut frozen bacon for soup, much to the amusement of houseguests.

The chainsaw gave us entry into a club of sorts. We know a guy who ran a two-person chainsaw, one of the first chainsaws ever made, an original from back in the forties when they needed a mule to carry the thing. It was worth it, he says with a grin, to do something the hard way to prove it could be easier. Another neighbor, Wally, a generous curmudgeon, kept a collection of saws, the cheap American ones you could buy at Kmart. The best saws are German (the Stihl) or Swedish (the Husqvarna), but Wally had neither. He had Homelites from the sixties and McCullochs from the seventies. When he died, his brother cleaned them and lined them in a row in the attic of Wally's shop, organized by the year of manufacture. A crowd gathered with beer by a campfire, and we took turns climbing the ladder to admire them. We nodded approvingly as at a museum display. Or maybe a wake.

Mostly the chainsaw got us *out there*. Bar oil stained my pants, and gasoline soaked my pack, and many nights in camp I picked wood chips from my eyes with a Q-tip and a handheld mirror. I slept tentless in the dirt and stared up at the sky where tree limbs crisscrossed my view of the stars.

From the outside, this is the irony that rankled most: how can you love this tool that kills what you love best? There's no easy answer, not for me, not for Wally, not even for Barnacle Parp. Not long ago, I picked up Parp's chainsaw guide, outdated now by four decades. I'd forgotten about his last chapter—or maybe I never read it. There Parp rails against clear-cuts and derides corporations and argues for better communication and tolerance between loggers and hippies. Barnacle Parp says what I have tried to say many times but could not for fear of sounding girly or sentimental. "This is a tool that can either take us further away from ourselves by increasing each individual's circle of destruction, or can help bring some of us back, close enough to relearn the language of the trees." He also says this: remember to take a break.

Maybe, in the end, that's all I've done. I've taken a break. It's not that I can't run a chainsaw anymore. If I want to start a saw right now, there's an 026 in the woodshed waiting, Sharpie-labeled with my name. But these days, I only use it for firewood, and I have lost some strength. After cutting firewood, the next day my spine walnut will swell, but it's worth it when the muscle memory kicks in, and the concentration, the Zen-like mindlessness, paying attention without paying attention. The chips fly, but I wear safety glasses now. There's no danger except my own weakness or fear or carelessness. The bucked rounds pile up around me, heartwood exposed.

And when I shut off the saw, I don't hear silence. I hear the absence of noise. I'm aware of every sound in the air: a squirrel taunting a housecat, a pickup rumbling down the dirt road, water in the river. After a while I hear only the wind in the trees like voices conversing, close and familiar and just out of reach, barely indecipherable. If I sit long enough, sipping water, stretching my back, I might make sense of them.

Winter Flood

HERE'S THE THING ABOUT THIS RIVER: ITS COLOR CHANGES seasonally, sometimes daily from silt gray to steel blue to latte. Then green, so many greens, a whole melted Crayola boxful—olive, forest, lime, emerald, avocado—bleeding one into the next, but not opaque, translucent like marbles, like Japanese glass buoys, like a wild cat's eyes. Penetrating. Unreadable. Changeability used to be something I admired, something mysterious and irresistible. In late spring and early summer, when snow—ten feet annually on the valley floor and more on the surrounding peaks—comes charging down, the river is a sporting one, whitewater class III, maybe even IV. Lupine and trillium line the banks. Dogwood flowers lean out over the water, shuddering. By fall, the river runs low, rocks shimmer from below, and Kokanee salmon spawn in the sand. Red-crested mergansers ride the riffles. The dippers, they dip. You get my drift. I love this river, I do. I also hate it.

Usually, in winter, the river runs lower yet, frozen near the banks and meandering midstream among snow pillows on rocks that lean out precariously, icing over then melting. Not anymore. Not today. I would not even be out driving today, would not even have stepped foot out of my house, except for the fact that Phil has cancer. He's one of a handful of close neighbors who's been diagnosed with cancer this lousy winter—another old-timer, Wally, is already bedridden—and when it comes to visiting a friend with cancer, you shouldn't mind a little rain, I know. This is not, however, a little rain.

I stayed inside for two days, wringing my hands. I had my excuses. Phil, after all, has plenty of other friends, friends who live closer to him, and besides there is nothing you can do about cancer. I figured I really only wanted to go visit for myself, for my own comfort, so I huddled inside, ostensibly writing, checking email, drinking in the early afternoon. A Ziploc bag with three novels he might like to read sat on the kitchen table next to a jar of homemade applesauce. Meager gifts to be. The rain fell, saturating the foot of snow we'd left unshoveled atop the woodshed roof after the last storm, growing heavier and heavier. How the shed could hold the weight I did not know. I half expected it to topple. Then, this morning, just after I dragged myself from coffee in bed, Phil's wife wrote to ask for help setting up an email list. At last! Something I could do! I didn't hesitate. I waded out to my pickup, started the engine, and headed down the road, which is, for lack of a better description, flooding.

It's not even river water, or not entirely. It's side creeks careening down the valley walls, spewing over the hard pack, and launching fire-hydrant style into the road. The accumulated current is moving fast, slush floating atop and a hard shell of white ice at the base, tire chain imprints visible through it all. The noise is deafening. I grip the steering wheel and hold my foot steady on the accelerator. What else can I do? I feel like a kid on an amusement park log ride or—check that, not nearly that fun—like a cartoon rat swept down a sewage pipe. The water clears the axles and seems destined for the floorboards. I lose steering and brakes and float toward the tight turns alongside a talus slope where I'll either get traction back or tip over the bermless edge into the river proper.

When I was younger and worked at physical labor all day, I'd pack a water bottle and a magazine on my day off and ride my bike along the road to a spot near here where in three or four short shivery strokes you could land on a gray slab of granite, roomy as a twin bed, worn smooth and slanting sunward. I'd lie on that rock for hours, reading or sleeping or staring at the sky, woozy and sated. Now that seems like a very long time ago. I sense my rear wheels sliding toward that very rock, and I steer with them, ever so subtly, to right myself, thinking, Nice spot, sure, but I don't want to die there. I find myself joking about death a lot lately. It's hardly ever funny.

At last I arrive at the house, just as my friends are packing for a trip to the oncologist and after that, to an alternative healing clinic in warmer climes. Phil does not look well: skin and bones, colorless and coughing, and he is not excited about leaving home. But he wants to try different approaches: diet, acupuncture, vitamins, anything. Anything at all. No matter what, he is not going down without a fight. Good, I say. That's good. I help a little with the computer. I set up the email list. I pet the Shih Tzu by the woodstove. There is really not much I can do, but at least I'm here. That's all I wanted to prove: No matter what, I'm here. And now it's time to go.

Only there's no way I'm driving three miles back home. Coming downvalley I was with the current. The other direction will be twice as hard. So I decide to ditch the pickup, and it's not a hard decision, hardly a decision at all, only a concession to reality. I go back inside to borrow a pair of too-long skis and too-small boots, and a daypack with snowshoes just in case. I am wearing sweatpants and the kind of shorty socks meant for joggers in San Diego or on a treadmill in a heated gym and the T-shirt I slept in with a light anorak pulled over it. But what else is there to do? When I came to this valley, I came with the plain wide-eyed wonder of a kid in a storybook, like stepping through the wardrobe into Narnia, like slipping through a Wrinkle in Time, like waking up in Oz. Did I fall so hard in love with the place because of the people? Or the people because of the place? The point is moot. I step into the three-pin ski bindings and begin the slog.

The berm is steep and slippery, and my feet in the thin boots are instantly soaked, but the skis are edged and hold me in place with each timorous step. And with each step, I fall into a rhythm. The cacophony doesn't stop. Rain spatters on my hood, the river roars to my left as loud as an airport runway, so loud I barely notice three deer standing on the berm in front of me. They know high ground and cede it wearily, unwillingly, dropping into the froth only long enough for me to pass. Then they climb it again. My heart is beating, and the going is good, or good enough, and my mind can drift as it only can outdoors, and there's something stunning—no matter how long you stay and how bad things get—about the whole of it: how clouds settle hard in the tops of cliff-rooted firs, how mule deer survive winters, and how water always, always finds its own way.

I ski back past the talus slope, thinking about how I sit by the river more rarely now, almost never. Not that I am busier, only less interested, or otherwise distracted. I took up windsurfing, a gear-burdened sport on the lake, a public exhibition. More often, I walk a former meadow near our home. When I moved here, the meadow was one of the few open spaces in the narrow valley: sunny and spackled with tiny shin-high pines. Ferns grew green in spring, browned over in fall, and collapsed. In one corner of the meadow, a patch of red poppies grew along the edge of dense forest;

over time, neighbors came to poach them, to plant them elsewhere, in proper gardens, before the river ripped their roots whole. As the river has. Most of the meadow is now cobble, but the pines, remarkably, have survived. They tower fifteen or twenty feet tall, skirted with debris and surrounded by sand. Sometimes Laurie and I think we should cut them and preserve this small preserve of sun. But we never do.

There's a television in the woods near the old meadow. It's a heavy wooden seventies console, tipped on end, a popular destination for teenaged friends and relatives who come visit. There are bicycle parts and drainfield pipe, shattered and choked by electrical wire, and blue tarps everywhere, wadded and torn. One cabin has had a cottonwood trunk jabbed through it for years now, jutting grotesquely; and right behind it, one summer, the river carved a perfect sandy-bottomed pool within the logjam. We skinny-dipped there without a thought. That's how used to it we are. Or think we are. Once we came upon some vinyl classical records, 78s, the titles in German, upright like javelins in the muck, and I began to sob. The records hit the nerve I can't touch anymore, one that's hardened over. I think of them now and ask myself: Does it hurt? Does it hurt?

I have tried not to picture the tumors. Normal cells gone berserk, growing large and combining for no decent purpose, for no damned purpose at all, attaching to pink healthy lung tissue and ballooning from there until the very life force that sustained you is killing you. Talk about

betrayal. Sometimes I overhear conversations that hinge
on deservedness: Wally smoked, but Phil never did. But at
some point that point's moot too. There's no parsing justice. The cells just keep reproducing willy-nilly, and these
strong men, aging yes, but vibrant and capable, accustomed to breathing outside air—a heady mix of pine and
fir, sweat and diesel, dogs and horses, cowboy coffee and
campfire smoke—eventually succumb to oxygen in a win-
dowless room. They cough blood under fluorescent lights.
Who deserves this?

The ski does not take that long. Within an hour or so, I
stand below our cabin and study the bank that holds us up.
I wonder: big rocks or small, strong roots or weak? I turn
to face the river. The water, for now, is even with the banks,
the flow itself is flat, no waves, the color is clear, the debris
minimal. Tire-sized snow clods zip across the surface and
back like air hockey pucks, fast and silent. I know the river
is coming. Maybe not today, but someday very soon. There's
no uncertainty about that. The road that skirts our property
will be moved behind the house, and then we'll be at the river's mercy. We'll buffer the bank with rocks and wood, with
willow plantings and a whole lot of cash. I'm not sure it will
make a difference. The river will win. I try to believe that I
don't hold this against the river, that this is not the reason
that I ignore it or disregard it, why the passion at least has
cooled. But surely it has something to do with it.

Sometimes I think of this river as a petulant teenager.
We set it free—no dikes, no dams—and back it comes, like

a drug-addled daughter, a stranger now, to steal from us, to rub our noses in it. You who loved most, you who are closest, you're going to suffer most. And not just the river. There are fires in summer and now this glut of cancer from god knows what: air pollution from China, mine tailings in the water, asbestos in the roof, pesticides ingested or solvents absorbed or plain wrong living. When I moved to the woods, I signed up for adventure and self-sufficiency, maybe even hardships—weeklong power outages, say, or wet sleeping bags in the woods—but not plagues of biblical proportions.

Here's what I'm thinking: climate change is like cancer. It's a dire diagnosis, maybe not yet terminal, but something very close, and it demands a kind of toughness, a fighting attitude, a willingness to change almost everything about how we live. People like to talk about this, to write articles and books and circulate petitions about the deserved-ness of it all—and the urgency—but hardly anybody talks about the flip side, about how beneath the diagnosis lies something else. The cold hard grief, for what we've lost, for what we're losing, for what we're going to lose inevitably, no matter what, and maybe most of all, for how we used to be—carefree and ignorant of consequences, full of youthful invincibility, yes, but also full of easy passion. And hope. I can't help it; I miss the hope.

I stand in the rain at the foot of the bank and pull back my hood, crying at last, though I rarely cry, and it's hard to know if it's even happening now. There's no way to differentiate tears from the cold rain on my cheeks, and since the rain has soaked the anorak and through my shirt, there's no way to wipe my face dry. Truth is, if nature is like us— diseased, in a way, due to fault and fate and nearing a kind of death—we're also like nature: not nearly as near to the end as we think. Wally will hang on for months before he goes; his brothers will sprinkle the ashes from an empty Folgers can on his potato patch. Phil will fight even longer: shoeing horses in the summer, cutting firewood in the fall for his son and his young family of six, newly arrived back in the valley, refugees from a decade as professionals in the city, wanting to give it a go. And we'll still be here. We'll be here by the river when it turns green, reflecting newness, and when it swells with gray glacial melt—too much, way too much—and when it goes shallow in the fall with drought—too little, way too little—and mergansers bob over ripples over salmon over rocks. I can say I hate this river all I want, but it's not true. If there's one way to show love, it's this: no matter what, I'm here.

Confessional Roots

THE SAME WEEK THAT JONI MITCHELL VISITED STEHEKIN—
under a pseudonym, wearing, I'd imagine, dark glasses
and oversize sun hat—I bought five of her CDs on a
whim. I heard a song streaming over the Internet, a song
I'd somehow never heard before, so gorgeous it made me
weep, and I thought: Enough! Enough feeling ashamed of
my obsession with seventies singer-songwriters, enough
fear of being a cliché, enough hoarding my money for
new releases from indie bands. I adore Joni Mitchell, and
I'm buying these discs, even if no one actually buys CDs
anymore. Making the purchase felt stubborn and self-
indulgent, but listening to that voice, so high and rangy,
so self-aware and self-lacerating—and unapologetically

self-centered—felt as liberating as ever. The very next day I went on a hike with a friend who gave me the scoop: Joni had visited with her adult adopted daughter. They'd kept their identities under wraps until the day they were leaving, and then they spilled the beans with the owner of the B&B where they were staying. Now everyone knew, at least everyone who cared, which turned out to be every woman in the valley over thirty. And I'd thought I was the only one.

Not so much about Joni. She's always been cool. Within a couple years of her secret visit, Zadie Smith would write an essay in the *New Yorker* about her passion for Joni Mitchell. Joni Mitchell has risen to goddess-like status among women of a certain age. But the other singer-songwriters I loved, the ones whose music—I may as well admit it now—shaped my life every bit as much as, say, Joan Didion or James Baldwin? Not cool.

Let's start with how very seriously I took John Denver. Sure, it was the round glasses, the boyish good looks, all gap-tooth grin and sun-squint, on the cover of his *Greatest Hits* album, the one album my parents owned as did the parents of every kid I knew, the one that defined the seventies as much as the *Brady Bunch* or Patty Hearst or Pixy Stix at Halloween. But that wasn't the whole of it. It was the music itself—the thrumming twelve-string, the straw-thin tenor, and, mostly, the lyrics: intimate and earnest, nature-themed and gently righteous, all children and flowers, mountains and sunshine. In my bedroom I harbored both a cheap stereo with oversize headphones and a soft-rock version of Catholicism—all guitar mass and Birkenstock Jesus—and my passion for Jesus conflated with my passion for John Denver, and from John Denver the passion spread and flowed, like a mountain stream, to others.

So begins my confession, with a partial list of the singer-songwriters of whose albums I owned three or more, on vinyl, before I turned eighteen.

John Denver (7)
Paul Simon, including Simon and Garfunkel (6)
Jackson Browne (5)
James Taylor (5)
Dan Fogelberg (5)
Cat Stevens (3)

I came to my allegiance a decade too late, parading in the streets of Southern California in 1985, the year of *The Breakfast Club*, wearing a ragg wool sweater and lug-soled hikers. At home in my bedroom, I strummed a nylon-string guitar and sang along to "Blossom," the opening track of *Sweet Baby James,* the fingerpicked bass line descending into a plain confession of loneliness. I was a nerd of the first degree, a freak not much different than the boys huddled at the lunch tables playing Dungeons and Dragons, like Ahmed, the only Muslim boy at our Catholic school, the boy who'd eventually take me to the prom.

Make no mistake, I had all the Beatles albums too and all the pre-1980 Springsteen. I dabbled in Miles Davis.

Even my favorite songs by any of the singer-songwriters were not the radio hits (not Fogelberg's "Longer," not even "You've Got a Friend"). They were songs that had a shadow of darkness or desperation and a glint of redemption (Jackson Browne's "These Days," Paul Simon's "American Tune").

I should be clear, too, that my interest in pop music was not lightweight in any sense. In elementary school, I had a manual typewriter and pecked out the title and artist of each song Casey Kasem counted down. I subscribed to *Rolling Stone* starting when I was twelve but preferred the cerebral Robert Hilburn in the *LA Times*. From him, I learned about X, about the Talking Heads, about Blondie. I listened to those bands but couldn't connect. There was a phoniness, a staged campiness, a clever sense of irony that I understood but shied from. Why did you need such ornate layers of complications: African rhythms paired with polo shirts, cowboy twang over punk chords? Such artsy tricks, I thought, were like the elaborate outmoded liturgy of the Latin Mass, designed to make something fancier than it is, to imbue a ritual with meaning, when maybe it doesn't need imbuing, maybe it's better without the obfuscation.

I wanted desperately to believe in a Utopian elsewhere—Heaven? Colorado?—in an everyday blue-jeaned Truth. In religion class senior year—Marriage and Family—I was paired with Ahmed. We did a compatibility test, and despite the facts of our different cultures, religions, and interests, we came up remarkably compatible. On a scale of one to five, how important to you is ...

Religion? Five.

Family? Five.

Money? One.

By the late eighties I was losing my grip. Like many people, I lost my religion sometime around the time I lost my
virginity. I left Southern California for college in Oregon
where I majored in English, signed up for English Roman-
ticism, and marveled at the obvious parallels. Shelley and
Byron, in playboy reputation, weren't far from Jackson
Browne. Maybe Dan Fogelberg was Keats—*Souvenirs* like
the Grecian Urn? Wordsworth as John Denver? That was
probably stretching it, but there were the same pastoral
themes. I even tried to agree with the professor, a former
hippie who begrudged the fickleness of academia for having abandoned the Romantics in the canon. (Parallels there
too. When had Robert Hilburn loved a singer-songwriter?
And *Rolling Stone* may have put James Taylor on the cover
as recently as 1980, but what album of his had last received
five stars?) But I couldn't quite.

I found Romantic poetry, well, bland. I knew this was
what people said about the singer-songwriters I loved:
bland and also melodramatic, often cliché. I tried to love
the Romantics, but the sentiments seemed to run shallow, though it's possible I didn't try hard enough, that I
couldn't unshackle my loyalty and missed the intimacy
of a lone acoustic guitar, fingers squeaking on strings
between verses. I lasted my four years, collected my degree,

and headed for the desert then the mountains. How many times had I listened to Loggins and Messina on the oversize headphones sing about living life near the rivers and trees? How many times? Too many.

Late one night a few years later, I was living in a moldy bunkhouse in the Cascades, working on a Forest Service trail crew, when Ahmed called. I hadn't seen him in a while, not since we played tennis on the courts at Caltech where he was getting his BS in electrical engineering that would be followed by a PhD in computer science while I collected a pair of matching degrees in the-language-I-learned-when-I-was-two. He asked what I thought about God. I didn't know. I hadn't thought about God in a long while. I told him I thought God was maybe Glacier Peak, the wilderness mountain we worked around, pink stained and conical, regal and sublime. He paused, then told me I should read the Quran and explained to me how the Quran says only a government led by a Muslim is legitimate. What was I supposed to say to that? I said it was late, said we should play some tennis next time I was in town. I hung up and went back to bed.

Once we'd all gotten over the giddiness of knowing she had been secretly among us, the women in the valley planned a Joni Mitchell night. We listened to her records and watched a documentary of her life. What surprised me was how many women, across generations, across even the political spectrum, had revered her. Some of the women explained that it was because she had been sexually liberating. I was skeptical. I'd just watched her famous Woodstock appearance on *The Dick Cavett Show* on Netflix, and there was nothing liberating about her. She wore a long peasant dress, as modestly covered as any fundamentalist Christian. Janis Joplin had been on the show the week before if you were looking for sexually liberating. And had they noticed Tina Turner?

What was sexually liberating about Joni? Words.

I knew that as well as anyone. "This Flight Tonight" had gotten me through several tumultuous flights and several tumultuous relationships. "Ladies of the Canyon" saw me through a season in Canyonlands. And in the first real breakup of my life, the hardest one, the one where you have to learn to steel yourself against the messy back-and-forth, into bed and out, came the line about the lover who claimed to be constant. Joni would have none of it. If he wanted her, she'd be in the bar. I was twenty-two. I could count the number of times I'd been in a bar on one hand. But the words gave me the strength to turn my back and leave.

According to lore, Kris Kristofferson told Joni, after hearing *Blue* for the first time, "Save something for yourself!"

If she had, we'd all be less.

Which brings me to my next confession: I published a memoir at thirty-seven. About living in the woods and building my own cabin. Cliché? Maybe. Stock singer-songwriter themes? Definitely. In the book, I blamed John Denver for my back-to-the-land venture, but that was not the only problem. My age was the problem. At thirty-seven, as many people will tell you unequivocally, you are too young to write a memoir. (In my defense, I didn't call it that. I thought I'd been writing *essays*, but the label stuck.) You're too young to be taking stock of your life, reshaping it into a simple unadorned narrative, and you're far too young to be telling other people how to do it. Not long after the book came out, I was offered a job teaching memoir writing online, and since I'd recently given up trail work, I snapped it up.

Even when I began, I suspected the trouble to come. I slogged through dinner party interrogations about how memory is unreliable, how dialogue can't be accurate, how this author condensed time and another conjured scenes. My position on those issues (in a nutshell: "don't lie") seemed irrelevant. The question served as a smoke screen for deeper annoyance: some people, many, dislike the idea of people writing about themselves. ("Save something for yourself!") The only thing worse, you might say, would be *encouraging* them to write about themselves. The presumption is that there's something self-aggrandizing about writing a memoir. The whole me generation thing, self-centered, like expensive yoga classes and trips to the ashram and eating organic for health, not for the environment.

I understood these arguments all too well because the same charges had been lobbed at the singer-songwriters. I'd read all about the teleology of the movement in the music reviews as a teenager. (I had to look up "teleology" and think hard about it.) The intensely personal music, critics argued, was a reaction against Vietnam and the ineffectiveness of the protest movement. Artists and listeners alike turned inward to nurse their wounds and came out the other side cockier than ever, the same way radical protestors became self-satisfied yuppies. I once read a review of early Paul Simon solo albums that claimed they exhibited "delusions of grandeur." I had to look that up too and think hard about it. Did writing about yourself sometimes lead to self-aggrandizement? Sometimes, I had to admit, it did. But not always.

So, too, with memoir. Yes, narcissism lingered around the edges of the online classes. Some students asked more about publishing than writing, but they didn't last long. Some believed, blindly—in a workshop, no less, with other memoirists—that their story was more unique and important than anyone else's. But that was the exception not the rule, and not the biggest problem by a long shot.

The biggest problem was fear. Aspiring writers feared telling any truth that might make people squirm. They dreaded the familiar label—"confessional"—one that I'd come to recognize over time was almost always saved for women. Stories of domestic abuse are often dismissed as "confessional" while war stories never are. (No one that I know of ever told James Taylor: "Save something for yourself!") Over the course of a decade, I taught hundreds of writers and learned exactly how widespread childhood trauma is. Not verbal abuse, but horrific physical and sexual abuse. At first I recoiled. I didn't want to read it, not once and certainly not dozens of times a day as the job required. But I was awed and humbled by the guts it took for writers to relive the trauma, and it did not take me long to realize that these stories must be told. Over time I became an advocate for the confessional, an ardent defender, a vehement one.

The charge of overearnestness is stickier. All you can say is the rule that applies to the memoirist is the same one that applies to the singer-songwriter: earnestness is not necessarily bland or cliché. Read, as evidence, Abigail Thomas, Edwidge Danticat, Kathleen Finneran, or Nick Flynn. (For that matter, read Joan Didion or James Baldwin. What is "Goodbye to All That" if not confessional? Ditto "Notes from a Native Son.") The list could go on and on. The unpublished stories, too, the unfinished ones, often showed seeds of brilliance and always showed courage. I loved reading those stories and loved helping the students hone them. If I had a flair for figuring out what worked, I have to think it's because of all those years of listening: I know a good confession when I hear one.

One last confession: I don't listen to seventies singer-songwriters much anymore. I couldn't even turn the music on as a background soundtrack to write this essay. I swoon occasionally with nostalgia when I hear it in a grocery store or a waiting room, but I don't rush to download it. Even by the late eighties, I was getting over it. I'd been loyal enough to buy some of the albums from the early eighties on cassette (*Lives in the Balance, The Innocent Age, Autograph*, god help us, *Vox Humana*). But I'd felt betrayed by the ornate orchestral arrangements, the drum machine, or the strident politics. I sold my albums for a quarter apiece at a record store in Eugene for muffin money. (I did not drink beer at the time, but I liked to buy one muffin a day from the cart on campus.) And I did not look back. Nowadays most of my singer-songwriter idols have seen their music resigned, mostly, to soft-rock stations that play in the dentist office or to the preprogrammed realm of satellite radio where they share space with Jack Johnson and David Gray. But—who knows?—maybe the dull middle is safer than the fringe.

Which brings me back to Ahmed. As a boy he'd had an easy smile behind out-of-style glasses and an easygoing sense of humor. He once won first prize in our annual literary club essay contest with an allegory, a story of a round ball and a series of square boxes, and there was delight in it, whimsy, enough for me to remember the story with admiration even if I can't precisely remember the moral. I knew, even then, his essay deserved to beat my own submission, a detailed description of popping pimples, which had no moral at all.

I Googled him recently. A few years ago, he moved to Saudi Arabia and earned a degree in Sharia law. Now he runs a systems company in Saudi Arabia. In the photo on the website, he smiles, and his eyes behind a long gray beard shine warm, intelligent, and intensely unironic. He offers this gently righteous recruitment statement: "We believe in remembering Allaah, working hard, and learning hard. We are looking for senior Muslim computer scientists from around the world who want to do good with their technical skills, and get paid well at the same time. We do not care about your nationality, color, or race except to say alhamdulillaah for what Allaah has made." It seemed an oddly inclusive kind of exclusion, and for a moment I wondered if he might hire women. Sometimes I wonder if Ahmed fell into some version of extremism precisely because he was once such a good, earnest boy, and as a once-good, earnest girl, this worries me.

All my life I craved authenticity. I hated cartoons as a kid. I preferred sitcoms like *I Love Lucy* and felt betrayed when I found out Lucy and Ricky didn't really share that New York apartment with the twin beds. It took me years to articulate what I'd known all along: there's nothing more inauthentic than authenticity. When memoir students debate how much they can fudge—the color of a bedspread, lines of dialogue in a long-ago argument, names or dates or locales—what they're really grappling with is this: how much fakeness is allowed when you profess to tell the truth? No matter what, on some level, aren't you always pretending to be honest? Aren't we all? You can't believe your own truth too much. If you do, it can lead to trouble. I've grown wary of righteousness, gentle or otherwise, especially in myself.

If I don't listen to the oldies, many of the so-called indie artists I do listen to sound suspiciously the same. Iron and Wine, Gillian Welch, Clem Snide, Damien Jurado, José González, Martin Courtney. Nature themes, navel-gazing, fingerpicked guitars, wistful soaring strings, occasionally a cello? Check.

But this newer glut of singer-songwriters seems self-consciously self-conscious, ever aware of their place in the larger scheme. They cover other artists the way rappers sample old-school soul. Bonny Prince Billy sings "A Man Needs a Maid." Mark Kozelek covers John Denver, AC/DC, and Modest Mouse. Earnestly. Gillian Welch does Radiohead; Iron and Wine does the Postal Service. They're careful not to box themselves in, careful not to appear to believe their own stories too much. I aspire to that kind of detachment almost as much as I distrust it.

I've written two more memoirish books since the first one. I can't seem to kick the habit. I have come a long way from the children and the flowers, and I'm a better writer for it, but I am careful not to play the irony card too often or to tease too much. I don't spend my extra cash on muffins anymore, but on cheap unironic cans of beer.

"Save something for yourself." The phrase haunts me. My students write fraught midnight emails fretting about it. Joni Mitchell once said of *Blue*: "At that period of my life, I had no personal defenses. I felt like a cellophane wrapper on a pack of cigarettes. I felt like I had absolutely no secrets from the world and I couldn't pretend in my life to be strong." A student recently called her journal an "eighty-nine-cent therapist," and I had to laugh. The albums of my youth were five-dollar therapists too. But it's not so self-centered as that. Unvarnished stories offer a window into lives unlike our own. Toward that end, I told myself I'd like to learn the story of Ahmed's life these past thirty years. I tried to contact him but found his LinkedIn account, his only online presence, available only in Arabic.

Here in the valley we sometimes talk about what will happen if Joni shows up again. We keep an eye out, of course, and once I thought I saw her. A woman in a white linen pantsuit (who up here wears a white linen pantsuit?) walking with a wide-brimmed hat and dark glasses, a scarf to protect her face. Sometimes, sitting around with friends, we wonder if that was her, or when it is, what will we do? Play her songs for her on a nylon-string guitar? Make her sit and listen? Wait! Wait! Here's another! Imitation not as flattery but as annoyance. It's good for a laugh in certain crowds, but it's not what would happen.

I should know. I met James Taylor once. It was at a remote ski area twenty years ago, a long story I'll spare you—in part because it already appears in one of the memoirs—but here's the gist. I told him, while we skied a long lap through a clear bright alpine meadow hemmed by aspens, that I'd always loved his music, that it had given me comfort and inspiration as a kid who'd lost a parent, as a girl struggling, unknowingly, with sexual identity. I told him his music inspired me to become a writer. I bared my soul as I almost never do in public. When I was finished, he said he was glad his music made a difference. He made eye contact. I could hear the practiced tone in his voice, the genuine attempt to sound genuine, to put me at ease. I know I've used the same tone with aspiring memoirists many times, in writing and in person, as they open themselves up, sometimes for the first time. I want to be encouraging, present. As real as I know how to pretend to be. If that's all I gleaned from hours spent listening to unplugged confessions, a tiny smidge of grace, well, it was worth the cost of cool.

So Many Rings

WHEN I WAS SEVENTEEN, MY LOVER'S WIFE FOUND A LETTER in his briefcase written longhand on college-ruled loose leaf—the same paper I'd used to take notes in his American government class only a few months earlier—a long letter, a manifesto of sorts, that consisted, according to her via him, of some profoundly troubling ideas about marriage. Thirty years later, newly married for the first time, I'd like to know what the hell I wrote.

Something in the "we don't need a piece of paper" vein, I'm guessing. I was the oldest child of a widowed-young mother and, more to the point, a child of the seventies and early eighties. What models did I have? The Waltons or the Ingalls, stoic husbands with strong subservient wives. Later,

the Huxtables or the Keatons, couples with yuppie accou-
trements who fawned over kids and swapped clever barbs.
I recognized the banter from swim team. Since we had no
pool at our high school, we borrowed another school's pool
and practiced after dark, flirting while we caught our breath,
chests heaving, between sets. The boys were shy and good-
natured with firm triangular bodies—broad shoulders,
narrow hips, tight butts, rippled abs—to admire through
the shimmery pool lights. But I couldn't imagine marrying
them. I couldn't imagine marrying anyone.

The seeds of what I didn't yet know lay in the shows I
loved best: *Mary Tyler Moore, One Day at a Time, Kate
and Allie.* Single women every one. When it happened, a
few years later, the brilliant hard fall, the swirling swoop,
my someday-wife and I were unprepared for what was to
come, how you have to come out, by pronouncement or
pronoun, not once but a thousand times: to parents, to
friends, to former boyfriends, to strangers, to landlords, to
employers, or not. Like the carnival rides that spin and rise
and drop and creak and do not seem up to the task. Those
rides smell like barf for a reason, not just the motion, but
the gut-lodged fear, real or imagined. I can admit it now:
the ride was scary as hell. Still, we strapped ourselves in for
the long haul. *Piece of paper be damned.*

But no, no, that wouldn't have been the whole of it—
the piece of paper argument—even at seventeen. My parents had been happily married except for one massive
screaming fight in the driveway over a too-expensive

Christmas roast that scared me enough to make me ask if they planned to get "'vorced," and they both assured me, sitting at my bedside, that they were never going to get divorced, ever. My dad died a couple years later. We had church friends who attended Marriage Encounter retreats intended to help couples "make a good marriage a great marriage." When as a teenager I worked as a motel maid at Howard Johnson's, the desk staff sniggered at the Marriage Encounter people smiling maniacally, arm in arm, recognizable from any distance. I could see their point: the couples' happiness seemed a gauze-thin cover designed to hide or forestall real trouble. With that in mind, it's possible the manifesto addressed impermanence. *Marry if you want, but don't expect it to last.*

I'm not sure I ever did.

On the side of the North Cascades Highway at an overlook above an unseen dam, we stood in drizzle to hash it out. Several months in, things had gotten tough. She'd been gone too often; I'd been too needy. We'd been on a road trip in search of early summer sun but had found none, and on the way home tensions had grown strangle taut. She pulled over. Cars whizzed by. Raindrops settled on my sleeves not wet enough to soak through. I dreaded what was to come. I was just shy of whimpering.

"Our real challenge," she said with a deep sigh, "will be to see other people."

I choked, and laughed aloud. This was the best she could do?

"No," I said. "The challenge will be to stay together."

Even she had to laugh.

On our fifth anniversary, while living in Flagstaff one winter, we bought rings etched with Hopi symbols—hers, the skier's, with clouds; mine, the swimmer's, with waves—and headed out for a sunset picnic with friends. Anniversaries, back then, commemorated the day we'd first held hands. The idea of marriage not just distant but preposterous. Ellen wouldn't even come out on television until a year later in a sitcom episode on which ABC placed a parental advisory. We didn't own a TV, so I listened to the controversy while watching a new neighbor try lamely to split firewood. The guy openly aspired to be a writer, which galled me. No way, I thought, could he ever make it. He couldn't even handle an axe properly. Whatever ideas I had at the time about authenticity or possibility or rightness applied more to splitting kindling or penning short stories than to getting married. Still, still, we had each other, and we had our friends, and we sat on a warm rock on a cold February evening and sipped box wine and fingered our new rings as orange sun splayed out over the Painted Desert.

The Internet will tell you that if your parents stayed married, you're more likely to stay married. The Internet will tell you the average age of a first marriage for a woman is twenty-five, which sounds too young, ridiculously young. I say this knowing full well how very young I was when we moved in together, twenty-three, but also knowing there was a critical difference: we weren't actually married. If you check the Internet for statistics on marriage long enough, you'll slip into muck, into quicksand explanations for why people like us should never be allowed to marry, ever. For more than two decades, we had disapproval as an omnipresent force, a reason to prove them—which sometimes felt, to me, like everyone in the goddamned world—wrong.

But disapproval didn't bind us anymore than approval binds couples that kneel at the altar. The omnipresent force is more mysterious and mundane, isn't it? She nursed me through knee surgery; I nursed her through a hysterectomy. She used to leave for work for eight days at a stretch. Now I leave for work, too often for too long. The push and pull. The push and pull. The sinking midnight frustration of hashing it out—where to spend Christmas or how to spend money or with whom we're spending time—trying to explain what's wrong, which is everything in the off-kilter universe, and nothing, nothing at all, as she begins to snore. The irrational anger, the desperation, a kind of drowning, must be a taste of what it's like to be a middle-aged wife unearthing a manifesto handwritten by your husband's teenaged lover on a topic she knows nothing about.

I lost my Hopi ring, the first time, in a high alpine lake. A friend in his seventies, the husband of a long-married couple, persuaded us to hike off-trail, to scramble over steep talus and through thick stands of face-slapping alder, up steep chutes strewn with loose gravel like ball bearings. We'd known people badly injured on this same route, but we agreed to go as long as another couple our age went along too. So we hiked, with one of the four of us, the youngsters, always losing our nerve, announcing in a loud whisper that we should really turn around. Our older friend never balked. We kept on until we reached the lake: the elliptical shape of an elderberry leaf, surrounded by tall glacier-smooth mountainsides, the water transparent mica, glass-clear and ice-cold. The sun was slanting low so we could only stay fifteen minutes. Just enough time for a quick dip. I dove fully clothed and arose gasping and realized my ring was gone. I could see where it sat atop a submerged rock ledge, ready at any moment to be swept by the current to the murky bottom, so I dove again—deeper than I like to go, ears throbbing with pressure—and surfaced triumphant with the ring in hand. We hiked down and crossed a river on a downed cottonwood log back to camp where the long-married wife awaited with a warm fire and thick steaks.

"Marriage" is a word without movement. Not a happening or a calling with that reassuring verb-like "-ing." Not a relationship or friendship, with a "ship" on the end ready to set sail. Marriage is static like a place (orphanage) or a state (bondage), like an action transformed into a process (passage or breakage), a scene turned summary narration. But a wedding is something else entirely.

When the law passed, we headed for the courthouse and got the piece of paper straightway and then sat in the parking lot at Safeway and called our friend, the judge, to see if she'd be available. She asked if we needed her to get a robe for the ceremony.

"We don't need the robe," I said.

Snow flitted off the windshield; shoppers hurried past.

"We need the robe," my almost-wife said.

The judge rode the chairlift gripping the robe in one hand and wearing a down coat with a hood. Other friends stopped to buy flowers and clutched them, too, on the lift. Snow fell in tiny beady flakes, the wind blew hard, the temperature hovered around twelve degrees. The old-fashioned lift, two seats with a bar between them, swayed as it rose over a spruce-lined creek and stopped, over and over, to let our friends, the non-skiers, off. My nearly wife and I stood and exchanged the rings we'd bought twenty years earlier beside the tiny midway lodge and then cut the cuffs of our long underwear to use as garters, cut a hank of every guest's hair and let it fly off into the trees, and drank pitchers of beer at bare Formica tables. When the sun began to wane, we rode the chairlift, coats zipped to our chins, with friends who'd tied cans to our bindings with colorful ribbon. At the top we gazed at rows of snowy peaks behind us, Mount Rainier glowing pink in the distance, and descended toward the blue Columbia River before us. We posed for a kiss beside the sign for our favorite run: Hidden Valley.

Love is love is love. If I could read my manifesto, I'm pretty sure, at some point, that's what it said. I don't think my seventeen-year-old self was entirely dumb. Pretty dumb, yes. Not entirely.

Marriage takes a thousand forms. My great-aunt Rose handwrote a memoir on six-inch-wide yellow loose-leaf paper of her arranged marriage at age fifteen. Her in-laws required a dowry of $500 and a chest of linens, and when her Italian father said no, just the chest of linens, they didn't come back for six months. She and her husband, a twenty-five-year-old barber, had "never talked together, never made our own plans" before their wedding day when a carriage pulled by white horses drove them away from the church and into Boston to live with his family where she "felt in a prison, doing all the work in the house." They stayed together for fifty years, and Aunt Rose lived alone, widowed, for twenty more. She is proud of her children and grandchildren. "Thank God I am in good health and crocheting," she concludes. "I love people and enjoy living."

Will it be different for us? Of course. There's no dogma delineating our roles. On the marriage license, the words "husband" and "wife" are exchanged for "Spouse A" and "Spouse B." Does that mean Spouse B will obey Spouse A? Or if we have kids, Spouse B will be expected to stay home? Does it mean Spouse A will make more money? I do not even remember whether I am Spouse A or Spouse B. We'd have to look it up. But how does anyone know how to behave? Who knows what goes on in the silence of another marriage? Maybe that's why people went to Marriage Encounter: to speak of what's not spoken of. As two women, we will be, perhaps, more accommodating, more forgiving, more sensitive. Which comes with its own challenges. For years we lived in fear of hurting one another's feelings, and that, too, kept us together. In the end, with no other map, we could do worse than to aspire to be like Aunt Rose: to love people and to enjoy living.

In line at the grocery store after getting our marriage license, the first gay couple in the rural county to do so, we discovered our picture on the front page of the local newspaper. In full color. We hadn't expected it. We knew a reporter had talked to us, knew a photo had been taken, but we thought the story would appear on, say, the back page of Section B. We tossed a stack of papers on the counter and watched the clerk who had been quite friendly turn merely cordial, and so it began, the public reckoning. Outside the store, there was communal euphoria in the air. Washington was one of the first states in the country to make same-sex marriage legal, not in a judge's chamber, but in the voting booth. Congratulations came from ferry captains and baristas, grade-school soccer coaches and online students. So, too, came the inevitable awkward stares, some from people who knew us well. Did it hurt? It did. The regular personal hurt: Aren't you happy for us? And the deeper sociological and moral kind: I don't get to vote on your love. Why do you get to vote on mine?

Then there was the other end of the spectrum. A dear friend, a gay man in a committed relationship, scoffed when the subject came up while we stood among a group of students. Activists had not fought all those years for such assimilation. Marriage? The military? How impossibly, infuriatingly, conservative! The movement was intended to be subversive. I backpedaled, changed the subject, and turned to accept the students' tearful best wishes. Sometimes it is like being a boat in a slip moored on either side. We're tethered to them, tethered against them—meaning, again, everyone in the world—suspended and stuck, buoyed and protected. There's no way it could be otherwise.

My wife lives in dread of me dying. If a movie steers anywhere near the topic, she goes to a dark place where there is no solace, and maybe I'd share her fear except that my genes suggest I'll be the first to go. Dad went at forty-eight, his dad at fifty-two. I hold this, admittedly, shamefacedly, as a trump card. I'll die first, I say, and laugh, try to make her laugh, but it is not funny, I know. We've watched it happen to too many of our married friends: an illness, an accident, a garden gone to weeds, woodworking projects left half-done, an empty rocker on the porch. I cannot even think about it.

We watch the geese. They arrive in hordes, and we count them, hoping always for an even number, knowing they mate for life, and wanting to be sure each has a spouse. For years, each spring, four of them have stood guard, facing me, four abreast, blocking the gravel road at a place between an open field and a fast-moving river—they must have nests nearby—as I jog past. They squawk and flap and disperse. This year there were only three, and one did not flee when I approached, just stood and stared. I cannot stop thinking about it.

Here's the truth: The manifesto was almost certainly bullshit, my way of justifying a sordid relationship, the only way to make a clean break, a fast break, a crucial break from the only home I'd ever known, a home held together by grief and by pushing against that grief. I did not know, then, how tenuous marriage is. Or I pretended that I did not. He presented me with a cheap gold band, an engagement ring of sorts that I wore in defiance of everything I knew. I knew, for one thing, even then, that he wasn't the only one at fault. Neither naïveté nor desperate opportunism is an excuse. I tossed the ring in the Willamette River at some point, in a fit of melodrama, but the damage had been done. I am sorry. I am sick and sorry for how I behaved. I do not even know if they're still married. I hope they are, though that probably has more to do with alleviating guilt than with faith in the institution.

On the day the Supreme Court struck down the federal Defense of Marriage Act (DOMA), I was at a conference teaching an oddly mixed group of older women and young college students, all earnest writers spending a fine summer day in a not-cool-enough classroom. One of them had written about her mother's death, about her love of music, and the rhythm of faith—Jesus, Jesus, Jesus. Some readers bristled and asked for the language to be toned down. We took a break. The college student sitting next to me, a competitive swimmer, checked his Twitter feed. I'd forgotten today was the day, the one that counted, really, more even than our wedding since DOMA kept me from being on my wife's health insurance. Now, here in the too-hot class-room, came the news that it'd been lifted, and all but one of the students cheered, not too loudly, not too much, toning it down because we had asked the silent writer to tone down her beliefs, and marriage, in that moment, seemed like faith, like music, like the stories we tell, to be both universal and intensely personal, deserving of respect. After the break, we got back to work. The swimmer had written about how he'd almost thrown in the towel, quit the team, seduced by equal parts rebellion and lethargy—who among us has not felt that way?—and how he came back to it, not for the competition, but for the ineffable pleasure, the feel of water against your skin as you move through. The rightness. The rightness.

I lost my Hopi ring, for good, in an airport bathroom. We'd been married two years by then, DOMA had been down for one. I left the bathroom ready to board the plane when I realized it was gone. I'd washed my hands thoroughly—it's an airport after all—and dried them with paper towels. I knew the ring was in the garbage. A stranger saw me weeping and helped me move the contents of one trash can, diapers and all, and put them in another. But we didn't find it. I heard the last call for my flight, and I decided to board. I have tried, ever since, not to think of it as an omen.

So many rings! There's the replacement one around my finger that binds the two of us, the circle of friends that sustains us, the small community we live in, and the wider world, too, like ripples in water or a bull's-eye on a target or maybe more like the interlocking rings of the Olympics logo. Getting married means announcing your place among all those rings, saying, essentially, Here we are! See us? But being married is something more subtle: accepting those rings as comfort and constriction, flexing within them and against them with as much grace and endurance and joy as you can muster. Like a late-day ski run or a very long swim. You can rest, but you cannot stop. You try not to get hurt. You ache and stretch and breathe and revel in the glorious world passing by for as long as you can last. Who knew you could do this? All married people must experience this, I think, though maybe it's harder for us. Maybe it will continue to be harder. If it is, on some level, I'll be grateful. As soon as things got easier, my ring was gone. Sometimes I worry that maybe I was not as vigilant as I had been before. Maybe now I expect things to stay a certain way. Which is how? What way? What, in the beginning, did I expect?

There's no way to know. All my journals are in the trash, tossed in a dumpster in a parking lot outside a Petco after collecting dust for years in mother's garage. My letters, hopefully, met the same fate. I have little affection for my seventeen-year-old self, and not much interest in her, but Joan Didion says we are best advised to remain on nodding terms with our younger selves lest they "come hammering on the mind's door at 4 a.m. of a bad night and demand to know who deserted them, who betrayed them, who is going to make amends." See, that's part of what I'm doing here, trying to make amends, trying at least to accept her, this manifesto-writing seventeen-year-old who did not know, who could not know, what was to come.

Sitting alone in a dorm room at yet another conference, I refreshed the Twitter feed obsessively, waiting to hear the Supreme Court decision, the final word, supposedly, on the legality of gay marriage, checking not because I need the legal protections so much anymore—though I suppose I'm glad enough to be able to move to Texas or Ohio if I want to—but to read the affirmations, to see the rainbow hearts. If the Internet is a mucky minefield, it's also a gathering space, and right then I wanted to be a part of it all and wanted, mostly, to be back home. I jumped in the car and drove fast over the green hills of the Palouse, variegated green and yellow-brown with irrigated and non-irrigated lands, with mowed lines like topographic contours rising and falling, NPR coming in and going out, the president, too, speaking and, for a moment, speechless with emotion. Finally back together, we pulled the shades to sleep late while the birds made their morning racket, and we woke to sip coffee in bed, just the two of us, until the DJ on the reggae station intruded to say: Let's celebrate together.

Yes, let's.

Breathe

IT'S NOT THE INHALATION; IT'S THE EXHALATION. YOU can pull oxygen in, but your lungs are already full with the wrong stuff, with all that CO_2 you haven't expelled. So you sip air. That's what the doctors call it, sipping. But that doesn't come close. Sipping is modest and moderate, shy, wise, sometimes coy, but never desperate. When you can't breathe, you're desperate. Coaxing air in through a sick fluttering wheeze and forcing it out in a staccato series of coughs. Then trying again. Not sipping air. Sucking.

I'd come home from fighting a forest fire coughing hard. Nothing new about that; you always come home from fighting a forest fire coughing, everyone does. Once I fought a fire in November, in subfreezing temperatures, where crews slept packed wall to wall on the floor of the local National Guard Armory—like displaced disaster victims, like contagious napping preschoolers—and came home with an annoying phlegmy cough that lasted until March. The TB fire, we called it, for tuberculosis. For years, whenever we ran into the grunts we met there on the line, we said, Remember the TB fire? And we laughed. Coughing, back then, was a laughing matter. Now I coughed from the core of me, an unworldly croak, like an elk cow in search of her calf, and it wasn't funny.

"Go see a doctor," Laurie told me.

I didn't answer. I didn't intend to go. I'd already decided there was little to be done, that I'd make a long expensive trip to the doctor only to be told to sit tight and wait it out. Take two aspirin. See you in the morning. That's what I expected. No solution I could imagine seemed workable. No solution seemed worth the cost. Wheezing, at any rate, did not seem the biggest problem the world was facing.

While I was off fighting that fire, airplanes had careened into buildings three thousand miles away, and the world shifted like continental plates beneath us. At home, too, the rules seemed to have shifted. This was now more than an annoying cough; my body was not recovering, not kicking back into gear. On the fire line we'd been digging in a frenzy, overturning sod on a dusty dry grass hillside, miles from the fire itself. When I stepped off the line to pee, from twenty feet away, I couldn't see the rest of the crew; but since it wasn't smoke but dust that was the problem, I didn't tie my bandanna around my mouth and nose. No one else was doing it. But when visibility drops below twenty feet, you ought to take that as a warning. Right then, on the fire line and at home, as in the world, all the important signs were missed. What would come next, no one knew.

The average respiration rate for humans is 16 breaths per minute. Multiply that times 1,440 minutes per day, and you get 23,040 breaths per day. Or attempted breaths. From where I sat, that seemed like an awful lot of work, an unfathomable struggle. It was best to stay calm, I knew, to conserve energy, not force your muscles to work and drain the blood of oxygen-rich cells and make it worse. Not even your heart. Don't work your heart, I told myself. But how can you stop that? You can't. By day, I went to work, hauling my pack and tools up the trails I maintained—firefighting was just a part-time money-making deal for trail workers like me—and stopping too often to catch my breath. By night, I sat, pillow propped in bed, staring out at the dark, not sleeping, not reading, not dreaming or philosophizing or even complaining. Just sucking air.

"You could die," Laurie cried, exasperated.

"No one dies of asthma," I said.

A week later, a doctor stood before me, hands on his hips.

"You could've died," he said.

I looked away.

"I had a twelve-year-old patient die of asthma last week. What the hell were you thinking? Way up there in the boonies? With no medical help? In a heartbeat, you could've died."

Asthma affects three hundred million people world-wide. Every day in the United States forty thousand people miss work, five thousand go to the emergency room, eleven people die. Eleven die! Every day! That means that since 9/11 tens of thousands of Americans have died a horrible can't-breathe death. If we're going to bother with war, why not a war on asthma? It'd be hard, I admit, in that weary-ingly familiar way: Who's the enemy exactly? Where can we point the bombs? Who the fuck is to blame?

Me, probably. That's what I thought as I sat in the clinic. This is my fault. Weren't kids with asthma milky cheeked and soft palmed? Weren't they the ones in grade school who had to sit out dodgeball? This I did not want to be. Never show weakness, my trail crew boss always said. By god, I did not intend to. If fire was no good for my lungs—a likely culprit in this whole rotty mess—it wasn't the only one. From down the hall, I overheard the doctors having fun with my X-rays while I sat half-dressed on the exami-nation table.

"Ever seen this?"

I leaned out to peek past the door at a small crowd of white-coated doctors gathered around the light screen in the central area for a little med school quiz.

"What do you call a lung mass like that?" my doctor asked, tapping the screen.

The doctors leaned forward and struggled with grade-school eagerness: Oh, I know that one. I know. It's on the tip of my tongue.

I tensed. Cancer? Please Jesus don't say cancer.

"Valley fever!"

The doctor returned to me.

"Where did you grow up?" he asked.

In Southern California. In the seventies. When we were kids, the air-quality gauge would drop below *unhealthy*, and we'd get smog days the way northerners got snow days.

Smog, then.

Except that Valley fever isn't caused by smog but by a fungus spore in the earth that, once soil is disturbed, rides the Southwest wind. More prevalent in inland places like Phoenix or Fresno, the spore can make it as far west as Riverside, apparently, but no farther. Not Los Angeles. Not even Pasadena. The sea air, the doctor explained, dilutes the dust and disarms it. And it didn't matter anyway. The Valley fever damage was done years ago, only the scarring remained, he said. Now the problem was asthma. Plain and simple.

But what had caused it? Was it dust or smoke or smog? Was it the cigarettes my parents smoked when I was a kid? Or the fires I fought as an adult? Was it our cat, Daisy, who I loved inordinately but to whom I was deathly allergic? Was it congenital weakness or plain dumb luck?

The doctor shrugged and prescribed inhaled steroids. Two puffs a day: morning and night. Two bucks a day. The wheezing, he said, should subside. The coughing should stop cold.

I wrote a check and went home, crumbled newspaper in the woodstove, laid in straight split slices of cedar, crisscrossed, and lit the match. The familiar orange glow reflected off the pine floors of my cabin and the pine board ceiling and the log walls, the flame and the tinder ridiculously close as always. I picked up Daisy and held her in my lap. I went back to work on the dusty trails. And despite it all, within a few days, my lungs were clear. I might as well have started smoking cigarettes.

By the time we'd gone to war with Iraq, I'd inhaled steroids every day for almost two years. So what if it was a problem with an uncertain cause? The solution, at least, seemed to be working. That statue of Saddam toppled; my lungs fell into step. I could run even. Run! If it took two dollars a day, that was cheaper than a beer or pot or coffee habit. It was also less than what I personally was paying for the wars in the Middle East.

So I sucked on my inhaler. My huffer, I called it. I used it morning and night. Since living in the woods had me somewhat suspicious of medicine, over time I tried quitting. But the sick squeeze in my chest, the watery wheeze, the inevitable croaking cough always sent me scurrying back. I knew I should try acupuncture or yoga. I should quit coffee and sugar and alcohol. Instead, I took a fistful of vitamins and exercised fanatically. I avoided stress, living in a gorgeous woodsy place, free of traffic and crime, with no boss, no children. Such low stress I should've just keeled over from boredom. I couldn't breathe without that huffer. With it, I could go running day after day along the dusty dirt road near our home.

When I was a teenager I ran cross-country. The air hung brown as the sweat ring on a collar, omnipresent, the same dirty brown as the drought-scarred foothills. But they told us: it's not what you can see but what you can't see that causes the trouble. Not the particulates, but the gases. Particulates, particulars, it didn't matter to us a whit. We ran up Mary Street on the sidewalk, under the freeway, into the orange groves, and then back, heading downhill toward school, toward snow-dusted Mount Baldy on the horizon— big beautiful Baldy—omnipresent too. Even when you couldn't see it.

Now there are summer days when you can't see the high jagged peaks that surround my cabin home for the smoke. Wildfires burn more often and more acres than ever, and the experts say it's a good thing they do. From my window, I can see an army of straight-trunked firs. Firs, firs, everywhere—not a single native ponderosa pine since pines require wildfire to regenerate—gray-trunked firs with dead limbs outstretched inelegantly as if in supplication. Many of them are dying, bug eaten or disease infested. Whorls of dry, fungus-caused growth hang large as haystacks. Witches' brooms, they're called, and even in imagination these would be awfully big witches. The forest is unhealthy. For lack of fire. We suppressed fire for too long, so now we have to let it back in. Fire is good! Fire is good! cry the forest managers. Problem is, for me, for my lungs, fire is bad.

It's all or nothing. That's the hell of it, isn't it? Win the war or bring the troops home. Put the fire out or let it burn. Use the huffer or wheeze yourself to death. Not because of politics or preference, but because that's reality. We want to live as we always have. We'll do our damnedest, yes, to parse the problems and do what's right. To a point. In the end we just want to breathe.

Truth is, in high school, I was a lousy cross-country runner. I performed more respectably on the swim team. I joined as a ninth grader who had spent hours splashing, diving, flailing in pools or in the ocean but who had never actually learned the technique required to swim competitively. The first time I tried to swim fifty yards, I came up panting, gripping the concrete lip of the pool at the YMCA, incredulous. How could people do this? How on earth did they breathe? By pacing themselves, of course, by pulling the air in and holding it for a long steady stroke, two, three, then expelling it slowly underwater before coming up again. The kids who'd been on swim teams their whole lives did this with ease. I was agog. They did not even seem out of breath at the end of five hundred yards let alone fifty. Not for the first time in my life, I was wowed by what patience and practice, time and training, could engender. I was humbled. After a year on JV, I moved up to varsity, swimming butterfly of all things, a stroke I'd admired since 1972, since watching Mark Spitz rise orca-like from the green chlorine depths on TV, then submerge, undulating. By the end of my sophomore year I could swim butterfly a hundred yards. Not only that. I could swim it faster than I could swim the crawl a hundred yards.

If you're patient, you hold your breath and you can survive anything. You can thrive. Maybe it's not all or nothing. Maybe it's pacing and practice, trial and error, plenty of error. The air is cleaner now, thirty years later, in Riverside. You can run the wide sidewalk down Mary Street for a mile with a calendar view of Mount Baldy. Even the evil unseen gases, researchers say, have dissipated. They fixed it with laws and science, research and regulation, a shift of behavior. Up here in the woods, there are prescribed fires—set in the shoulder seasons of spring or fall when the conditions are right—that can mimic the work of wildfires, clearing underbrush, setting pine seeds free, making the forest healthier and less likely to get blackened in a catastrophic burn. In the wider world, there are diplomatic negotiations—tedious and trying, requiring humility and compromise, heartburn and exhaustion on a grand scale—that have brought tenuous peace in Ireland, in the Balkans, maybe someday in the Middle East. I try to be hopeful, I do.

The label on my steroid prescription warns me that it might cause the following: headaches, dry throat, infection, depression. Some of my friends believe that's not the worst of it, just the tip of the iceberg, what the drug companies are willing to admit.

I called a doctor friend to ask outright: "Is the inhaler going to kill me?"

"Wheezing will kill you faster," he said.

Maybe, I think. Maybe not. I have no way to know. I only know that I remember those nights awake sucking air—the terror, the desperation—and those memories haunt me.

Another memory. I stand waiting for the gun. One-hundred-yard butterfly. At *take your marks*, I'll bend forward and clutch the slanted platform at my feet. At the gunshot, I'll arch up then dive shallow and surface in motion. But for now, in the interminable seconds atop the starting block, I'm terrified. Nothing short of that. I'm convinced that I won't make the full one hundred yards. The sheer physical feat seems impossible—implausible!—even though I've done it a thousand times, and I'm certain, absolutely sure, that I'll flail gasping and have to call for help in shame. I can conjure that whole scene more easily, much more easily, than I can imagine what will really happen, which is this: I'll dive then take two strokes head down, one head up. The head-up stroke will take more energy, since I'll have to pull my torso out of the water. For the first fifty yards it's not hard, not at all, but as the race goes on, and my lungs burn, I'll try to breathe too soon, jerking my head up a millisecond before my abs have lifted my shoulders, and I'll take water into my windpipe. I'll choke. I choke— actually, literally—every single time I race butterfly in high school. And once I begin to choke, I swim much faster. In the end, that's the only reason I am worth a damn at all on the team: because I am swimming for my life. Swimming freestyle I am trying hard, but I am sated; it's too easy, nothing at stake but a plastic trophy and my pride. Swimming butterfly I crave air, and I'll do anything to get it. Turns out, if you want to win races, that's a good thing.

Just recently I made some progress. I cut my steroid dose in half. I tried quitting whole hog again with predictably bad results, so I scaled back to mornings only—one buck instead of two—and wheezed some at first, then less over time, until anymore there's only a hint of struggle when I linger too long in bad air: shoveling ashes from the woodstove, say, or jogging behind a school bus on a gravel road or idling in traffic. Laurie is, so far, wary. The doctor advises against it. Me, I want to stick with the experiment not so much because I believe things will get back to how they were—breathing free—but because it feels right. For so long I've been trying to tell myself that everything is fine, just fine, that we are, all of us, doing the very best we can, but there is, in me, beneath the salve of the huffer, a hint of uncertainty. There is always, with every inhalation, 23,040 times a day, an edge of panic. I'm thinking that's a good thing.

The Fiddler on the Rock

RIDGETOP MEADOWS STRETCHED OUT SILENT, OR MOSTLY so. A chipmunk rustled beneath pink-flowered heather. A marmot whistled from behind a rock in the sedge. To my right, a steep, red-stained mountainside rose against blue sky where a hawk soared and cried. To my left, green forest dropped to a valley cleaved by a raucous river, a river so fast and loud you could hear it from six thousand feet above. Thirty miles and three days from a trailhead. Just me alone with my thoughts.

Which weren't terribly lofty. What would I have been thinking about? The weight of my pack or the distance to camp? Maybe. The book I'd recently read, set right there on the ridge, about a clash between a miner with a claim on the iron-stained peak and an environmentalist who opposed it? I doubt it. Friends far away, romance woes, career choices? Likely. I was preoccupied that way, it seems, nearly all the damned time. I was fresh out of college, working in the woods, lost in a way, found in a way, trying to figure things out.

Then it struck. A loud noise, a deafening noise, maybe the loudest noise I'd ever heard. No animal scream, no giant tree crashing, no glacial calving, no matter how loud, sounds like that. Not even trail blasting—regular dynamite explosions—howled like this, metallic and swooshing, and bam, boom, shaking the whole wide world to the core.

I fell to the ground, covered my head, and waited to die.

Who wouldn't? The Soviet Union was still the Evil Empire. Just barely. The nuclear clock ticked, had been ticking in fact as long as I'd been alive. In recent years friends had attended No Nukes rallies and Beyond War meetings, but none of that made a difference. The nuclear clock just kept ticktock ticking, year in and year out. I'd always known I'd die in a radioactive blast. We all would. I just hadn't expected it to happen in the wilderness.

I lay on the ground, nose in the dirt, and waited.

Over time, I'd learn to accept that noise as part of the landscape, predictable in its unpredictability. It was an airplane for god's sake, nothing more, a fighter jet going faster than the speed of sound, leaving a sonic wake, a sonic boom, and by the time you heard it, the jet was long gone, out of view. Over time, I'd learn to see them too. Someone must've taught me the trick: when you're on a high ridge, look down, not up, since the pilots fly below ridge level, navigating tight river valleys like a real-life simulator, like a war game without the war. They were not supposed to do it, no, but like many things that happen in the name of national security, they did it anyway.

For now, I was alone and grateful, if a little baffled. I stood and brushed myself off, shouldered my pack, and moved on.

I went home to a house full of other eager young people from all over the country. One housemate, a woman with long braids and an easy smile, played the violin, the "fiddle" she insisted, but she played it with more nuance and skill than any fiddler I'd ever known. While the rest of us patrolled trails or harvested native seeds, she was assigned, to her dismay, to sit on a rock and watch for planes flying overhead—or below the ridge depending—so she could write down the tail numbers, so the land managers could contact the naval base and complain, so the overflights would stop or be limited. A noble plan, but a very boring job for my housemate. Day after day she'd pack a lunch but not a book; if you're reading, you're not watching and you might miss a flight. She grumbled at first, but after a while she seemed to adjust, maybe even to enjoy the duty, and I could not figure out what had changed. Zen acceptance? Earnest faith in the master plan? Who knew? Me, I avoided plane-watch at all costs.

Not that I was unfamiliar with military aircraft. I'd grown up near an air force base. Dads of kids in school flew B-52s, and for field trips we'd tour the massive bombers, the size of our portable classrooms. The planes in the woods weren't B-52s, more like the Blue Angels or the Thunderbirds, the military demonstration teams, the show teams we'd go watch at festivals or parades, whose fast-spinning tumbling-speed grace was matched only by the astonishing ear-splitting roar. I did not pin up posters of those planes on my walls, few girls did, but I didn't dare grouse about them either. They were part of the world I inherited, the world I left for college, then after college, for the wilderness where every weekend I'd walk up a trail and just keep walking only to learn, as we all learn, that you can walk as far as you want, but you can't ever escape.

Often on my days off I hiked near the place where my housemate was stationed to watch for planes, not on a trail but a ways off on a rock above a waterfall with a clear view. One day as I passed nearby, I heard another sound that cut to the quick, higher than a varied thrush, sadder than a steady rain, more joyous than a walk in a silent sun-soaked meadow, swelling, bursting, swirling. The fiddle, of course. I dropped my pack and wandered a bit hoping to find her, to catch her in the act—no wonder she loved the duty!—but I could not. She was out of view. I sat alone mid-trail and listened.

You think you don't want to hear anything human, ever. Then you do.

That was twenty-five years ago. The Evil Empire fell, fear of terrorism rose, wars were fought. Soldiers came home as veterans to work in the mountains, shaped and sometimes saddened by what they'd seen. The flights still come, more rarely, but always unexpectedly. The last sonic boom I heard was from inside my cabin. The walls shook and the picture windows in the living room bowed and released from the pressure. Birds fly into those windows, sometimes, too. We hang netting to urge them away, but still we find their bodies limp on the ground. Or the cat does.

We are trying our very best. We are still causing harm.

Sometimes I think I did not hear the sonic boom on that particular ridge on that particular day, only that I've heard sonic booms in the wilderness so many times that the memories have blurred into one. The fiddle is different. In my memory I've heard it time and again, every time I've passed that place—hundreds of times—and I've pictured the fiddler out on the rock, her braids swinging, her bow arm flying, her easy grin grinning. But the truth is I never saw her, and I heard it only once. And I never forgot.

When We Talk
about Courage

ON MARTIN LUTHER KING JR. DAY THEY FLOCK INTO THE
room. Kids and adults, black and white, and bored, exuberant, and curious. It's free admission day at the Washington
State History Museum in Tacoma. While rare winter sun
reflects off wet sidewalks and clouds swirl against wide
swaths of blue, inside the remembering begins. I'm here
to tell stories about unsung heroes and sheroes of the civil
rights movement. So many of them, stories about bus seating protesters that I learned while doing research about
my dad's small role in the movement. I'm excited. I've put
together a slide show, and I've rehearsed the stories, and

still I'm unprepared for my unease as the crowd files in and the lights go down.

I take a deep breath. It's not just the big names, I say, not just the stories we know. I flip through slides trying to give voice to courage. Here's young Irene Morgan who refused to give up her seat on a Greyhound in 1944—eleven years before Rosa Parks!—and took her case to the Supreme Court. She won. Here's Claudette Colvin, the feisty teenager who took a similar stand on a city bus in Montgomery seven months before Rosa, nudging the movement forward a step or three. And here are Wilhelmina Jakes and Carrie Patterson who were arrested in a bus seating incident as college students in Tallahassee, Florida, in the fifties. When the Klan burned a cross on the lawn outside their dorm, the bus boycott in that city—the one my white father later participated in—began. I pace my voice, try to make the stories as thorough and miraculous as they can be in a few short minutes. The audience listens, these good people. They are wowed. They have come to learn about how far we've come, about the victories we've achieved, and I am glad to fill in those blanks, but something is nagging at me.

Nixon lied. Sharon Ryan pulled her station wagon into the driveway and hopped out with the engine running. "He erased the goddamned tapes," she yelled. I was five. Iran-Contra broke while I sat in a college class called Crisis in Central America. The professor announced it, body shaking with rage, and we thought he had finally and completely lost his mind. We were sure he had made up this elaborate paranoid scheme. He had not. The Berlin Wall fell while I camped in the desert. When I saw the headline a week later, I thought it was someone's bad idea of a joke. What I'm trying to say is this: When you take in Watergate when you're five, you learn cynicism by osmosis. And it's hard to shake.

Downstairs, before my speech, an actor played the part of a child activist, reading a dramatic script while behind him film footage from Birmingham and Selma and Montgomery flickered on a big screen. Some of it was hard to take. Marchers, many of them children, approach fire hoses, nightsticks, tear gas. They move forward toward the danger and forge on into the heat, into the very heart of it, beaten and bloody, maimed and stooped and sometimes crawling. Why so much violence on a day set aside especially to celebrate its antithesis? Why the warlike subtext? In my own presentation I flip to a newspaper photograph of a Klan rally—men hooded and faceless, crosses aflame—and take another deep breath. I tell myself there's no way around it.

In high school, we attended Holocaust Awareness Day annually. Check that. We were dragged to Holocaust Awareness Day at a local synagogue, a horde of Catholic teenagers overcome, year after year, with dread. We dreaded the speeches, the prayers, the gravity and solemnity, and, most of all, the black-and-white film footage of chain-link fences and emaciated bodies, the piles of bodies. We could not take it. We tried to ridicule the stories; we made lame jokes. We also wept. If we thought it was cruel for our teachers to bring us here, unfair, we also had to keep our complaints in perspective. Cruel? Really? Unfair? Compared to what? For the rest of my life, those days will haunt me. When I grew older and heard the unending stream of commentators rage against Holocaust commemorations—Why not the Native American genocide? Why not Stalin's Russia? Aren't we forgetting Rwanda?—I took it with a grain of salt. No need for comparison shopping. The setting might be different, but the message is the same: Never again.

Never again what?

I flip to another slide, not a newspaper headline this time, but an actual photograph from a Klan rally in Tallahassee. There is no atrocity here, no baton, no nooses, nothing aflame. On one side of the screen is a lone Klansman. He wears the white robe, which hangs past his knees, and he wears a half smirk on his face, as one hand reaches for the pointy hood to pull it finally down. He looks easy, comfortable, as if saying to us across the decades, What? What are you looking at? On the other side of the screen is a crowd of festive white folks. A man in dress pants lights a cigar, a shirtless boy stands hands on his hips, a mother cradles a toddler in her lap. There are sulking teenagers, men in hats, women in dresses, grandmothers even—all of them, to a one, looking eager and attentive, as though awaiting a fireworks show on the Fourth of July or a parade.

Never again what? Never again go along to get along.

In the corner of the screen is a young boy. He's the only person in the photo who looks uncertain. His hands grip the single strand of barbed wire that separates the crowd from the Klan, and he gazes askance, off-camera, as if considering an escape. Go, I want to say. Get the hell out of there.

I doubt he will. Long before I ever attended Holocaust Awareness Day, I knew all about going along to get along. Who didn't? We were in high school, for god's sake, and the whole point of high school is to go along to get along. And it didn't end in high school. These days I'm a gay woman living in a very small rural town, a Democrat in a bright red county. Like adults everywhere, there are times I have to go along to get along. Plenty of them. If I didn't, my life would be hell.

Next slide. We're back with the heroes: the bus riders, the lunch counter sitters, the marchers and their everyday acts of defiance, building one on the next, over years, decades. These are rousing stories, so exhilarating, and I can sense the museum crowd getting on board, so to speak, being moved. Who wouldn't be? And isn't that why I've come? We love to feel a part of it. We're spectators on the sidelines, delegates at a political convention, kids at a pep rally, fans at a rock concert with lighters flickering, hoping for an encore, screaming our throats raw. One more. Just one more. How does this collective river spill over the dike from exuberance to irrationality? From nationalism into genocide? How do you see that line? Where do you learn?

CYNICAL: Def. 1. believing that people are motivated in all their actions by only selfishness; denying the sincerity of people's motives and actions.

Clinton lied. Enron collapsed. Bush was elected. Sort of. Maybe I am not cynical. I am skeptical. About penitent speeches penned by publicists, about press releases submitted by campaigns or marketing departments. About the efficacy of the stock market, the neutrality of the judicial branch, the ability of men—and women, too—to make and keep commitments. To be steadfast.

Next slide. Here's C. K. Steele, leader of the Tallahassee boycott. "I'd rather walk in dignity than ride in humiliation," he said. C. K. Steele, father of six, who, when his living room windows were shot out by thugs, left the bullet-scarred blinds hanging for decades so everyone would remember. C. K. Steele, who was arrested with eleven other boycott leaders for running an illegal carpool, proceeded to preach several sermons every Sunday for the rest of his life to pay the $11,000 in legal fees. Did they achieve victory? Eventually, yes, but not right away. Bus segregation remained legal, on the books at least, in Tallahassee until 1972—for fifteen years after the boycott—but never did C. K. Steele waver. Not once. He was steely, I tell the crowd. He knew what was right and stood for it.

But I worry about this message, too, how it can be twisted to level the playing field of oppression, to flatten it to meaningless. The landowner who can't log the trees from the banks of a salmon stream is oppressed. The woman in line at the emergency room behind an illegal immigrant is oppressed. Righteous indignation does not hinge on righteousness. Even protest seems suspect, fair game, co-opted. In Spokane one spring I stumbled upon a lively rally—chants and speeches and citizen activists—featuring posters of President Obama with a Hitler moustache. What did they oppose, these sincere people? About what were they so defiant? Paying taxes.

CYNICAL: Def. 2. sneering, sarcastic.

The indie band Luna sang a bouncy pop song about Nixon in a coma. I used to listen to it a lot. Now, in Tacoma, I can't get the song out of my head. Is it pop culture that makes me cynical? It is not.

Here's a slide I don't show: a Greyhound bus aflame on Mother's Day in Anniston, Alabama, 1961. I don't show it because it's not exactly relevant and because I'm not sure I can maintain composure. The bus had been carrying Freedom Riders—white and black volunteers riding together, integrated, testing that Supreme Court decision from 1948, the one Irene Morgan instigated. The laws had been on the books for thirteen years but were rarely if ever enforced. Especially in the South. The crowd in Anniston, a well-dressed after-church crowd, stopped the bus and threw gasoline-soaked rags through open windows. Then a match. "Burn the goddamned n—," they cried. Whites and blacks alike debarked safely, sweating and coughing, before gas tanks exploded. In photos, descending the steps in suits and ties, the Freedom Riders do not look dissuaded. They look tired and a little frightened. Soon, a new bunch will board another bus and continue. It's not the Freedom Riders who hold my attention in the slide. It's the onlookers, and one in particular: a woman smiling so wide, laughing really. Her lips are pulled back from her teeth and gums, like a mule. A hideous mule. Sometimes I want to kill that woman. Then I think about what made that woman want to "burn the goddamned n—." Same urge.

How do you tell a room of children about these things? How do you tell them all they need to know? Be what you want to be, be bold, be brave, but also be discerning, be compassionate. Think before you join. Consider the consequences. Fight oppression, but also prevent oppression. How, especially, when the potential for cruelty is within us?

I have scanned my own heart in search of that woman with the mule-lip laugh. I have told myself, genuinely, that she's not there. But it's not true. When I was in third grade, I led a small band of bully girls. The Gorillas, we called ourselves, and we chased after a smaller group of fat girls. We called them names, to which they replied, "Sticks and stones may break my bones," which further enraged us, so we yelled some more and chased them harder. Why? Just to see them run? If so, then why did I hit them? Because I could. I remember the moment I realized I could get away with punching them. I was, in fact, getting away with punching them. Power welled like adrenaline. I was more athletic than these girls, physically stronger, and a goody two-shoes besides. My teachers would never suspect me.

I know. I know. It's not the same: playground meanness, the killing fields. But where did the urge come from? I was a well-loved child. I've got no excuse, sociological or psychological, for leading the Gorillas' charge or, more troublingly, for the way the memory has lodged so hard in me: the grassless playground gravel and the traffic beyond the chain-link fence and pudgy girl-fisted blows glancing off me, ineffectual, and the look on my victim's face of disbelief and disdain and disgust. All of it, every aspect, excited me more. See? I do not distrust my sincerity. I distrust human nature, including my own, which can, on so many occasions, be sincerely fucked up.

Maybe my problem is nothing more than birth timing, a Gen X thing. Maybe there is a new generation, unscarred, oblivious, who will carry the MLK Day message, unsullied, forth without nuance or incessant irony or complication, to a place that spawns action and discretion in equal messages. I hope so. I sincerely do. But I am skeptical. Part of me thinks maybe when you learn cynicism by osmosis you are better prepared to parse the truth.

We are winding down. I tell the crowd how the local newspaper, the *Tallahassee Democrat*, suppressed news of the bus boycott in that city, that it was, in fact, one of several southern newspapers to issue apologies, fifty years late, for having purposely suppressed news of the movement, to keep it from getting too big, from getting too much media attention, yes, and also to avoid condemning subscribers. The editors thought doing so would be like tugging on the threads that held the city together, pulling the very fabric apart, starting the unraveling. A necessary tugging, we can see in hindsight.

Next slide. Does anyone recognize him? No one does. Congressman John Lewis. Veteran of the March on Washington, Freedom Rides, Freedom Summer, arrested more than forty times, beaten unconscious by state troopers on Edmund Pettus Bridge on Bloody Sunday, March 7, 1965. Since 1986, he has served in the U.S. House of Representatives. I admire John Lewis. I revere John Lewis. I trust John Lewis. And now I have to follow in his footsteps, do a little tugging of my own.

I continue: In 1996, as Congress debated the Defense of Marriage Act, the anti-gay marriage act, Congressman John Lewis said, "Marriage is a basic human right." He also said, "I have known racism. I have known bigotry. This bill stinks of the same fear, hatred, and intolerance. It should not be called the Defense of Marriage Act. It should be called the defense of mean-spirited bigots act."

This is not the story I was invited here to tell, and my motives are both sincerely selfish and sincerely selfless, and it's such a small stand as to be hardly worth it. But I say it. Then I pause. The room is silent.

I am not so much cynical as afraid. I stand in front of a room of people telling stories about courage, but I am afraid. Afraid the civil rights movement did not accomplish enough. Afraid what it did accomplish will erode. Afraid of how reactionary forces held sway in this country for nearly a century after the Civil War, and how they hold sway now.

Next slide. There's my dad who sat beside a black man on a bus and got arrested to test a lousy segregation-saving law in Tallahassee back in 1957. A very small stand. My dad died young, yes, so he couldn't tell me about it, but—next slide please—here are his friends, Johnny Herndon and Jon Folsom, who told me their stories of courage and his. How they received hate mail and couldn't find work and had to quit college for lack of funds. How thugs shot holes in Jon's car. How the cops picked Johnny up in a new wool suit and made him work the chain gang wearing it until it was tattered.

Your father, they said, was a brave and good man.

Where do you learn?

You don't learn from the television. You don't learn from a pop song. You don't learn from a newspaper headline.

He stands behind me now, my long-dead father who took a small stand in a lifetime of small stands, in a slide show alongside a dozen other heroes and sheroes who took small stands, while I stand in a room with a hundred people who have, no doubt, taken their own small stands and will take them again, and who have brought their children to hear stories. The children, we all hope, will learn to speak up, to vote, to attend rallies, to sign petitions, and to watch carefully, vigilant always, for what can rise up within them and without them.

Next slide.

Where You'd
Rather Be

ON WARM SUMMER EVENINGS AFTER WORK I USED TO SIT
on my porch and visit New York City. The porch, I should
note, is surrounded by forest. A glacier-fed river runs a few
hundred yards away. Steep granite cliffs rise closer than
that and keep on rising into rugged wilderness, nearly
three million acres, right from my backyard. Sure, sure, it's
nice, but come happy hour with an icy cold beverage and
a magazine in hand, I was not interested. I was off to a city
three thousand miles away.

Of course it wasn't real. New York on my front porch
consisted of book readings and concerts—only by authors

or artists I adored, the others I skipped over—and hip new delis serving dishes I'd never eaten and could never afford and cultural profiles and political analyses and cartoons I did not get. When I did get the cartoons, I cut them out and scotch-taped them to our washer and dryer in the bathroom. Little souvenirs of my nightly trips. The dryer is ragged with them.

Until a few years ago, I considered it my personal challenge to go through life as a bookish American without ever seeing the place. Just as, before that, I swore I'd never subscribe to the magazine. That fop with the top hat on the cover? The stories of yuppie angst? I had no use for them. But after a decade carrying too-heavy paperbacks or worse, ripping them into sections to carry into the backcountry—*Anna Karenina*, on my shelf, consists of five separate sections rubber-banded into one—subscribing to a word-dense weekly began to make sense. From there the descent began. I flipped to Talk of the Town first thing, anticipating Hendrik Hertzberg like a hot new crush. I picked up Joseph Mitchell's *Up in the Old Hotel* and loitered in the Bowery, then Phillip Lopate's *Waterfront* and soaked up development schemes and architectural theories, labor unions and Rollerbladers, none of which can be found within, say, a fifty-mile radius of my front porch. I crossed over into Brooklyn with Jonathan Lethem, *Fortress of Solitude*, adding the supernatural and the Talking Heads as soundtrack. I sank deeper and deeper into a place distant and exotic and, after a while, familiar.

I wasn't the only one. A carpenter who lives a half mile down the dirt road, and has for over thirty years, spends most of his time in New Orleans. Way before *Treme*, he was hooked. As soon as Internet arrived in the valley, in the early aughts, he tuned into WWOZ and, well, turned on. He'd once been addicted to Grateful Dead music, but that was years before, almost a lifetime. Now he grew obsessed with Kermit Ruffins and the Nevilles, with Irma Thomas and Little Freddie King. On his jobsites, where I sometimes helped out, he played cassettes of OZ shows recorded from the Web, complete with weather forecasts and local event calendars. One late August, as early snow settled on the peaks, he listened to news of Katrina like it was happening next door. Devastated. On long Mardi Gras cross-country ski jaunts, he brought multicolored plastic beads for us all to wear. Elated. He'd never been to New Orleans until he made it to Jazz and Heritage Festival a couple years ago, but he lived there anyway.

I know how this must sound, like we were somehow deprived, my neighbor and I, starved for human contact. That's not true. Our valley may be small, but social life is lively, in summer especially, and neither of us grew up here. He's from St. Louis; I'm from outside L.A. The attraction wasn't deprivation, I'm telling you—there's no way we would've stayed so long if that were true—but imagination. Those summer evenings on the porch took me away. When, in the morning, I'd wake to another day of the same hard labor on the same steep trails or, later on, to the same essays from different writers, I'd mind less. I'd see some spark, some new angle of light or turn of phrase. This is the argument people make for travel, isn't it? The broadening of horizons. The changed-ness. So, too, with travel in your dreams. It's cheaper for one thing, and if Internet ads are any indication, my neighbor and I are not alone. Sidebar beaches flicker on the screen midwinter beside emails and editorials, and I picture the whole lot of us, office workers in New York, housewives in Seattle, wannabe writers out in the boonies, all transported briefly to our own private Caribbean. I suppose I could find that image depressing: the mutual longing, the dissatisfaction inherent, the marketing that spawns and spurs it. Instead it delights me.

Some evenings while I read on the porch, I would hear tourists passing nearby on bicycles. They sounded happy. They were on vacation, and many of them had, apparently, never seen a place so wild, so exotic. And yet so familiar. After all, you can inhabit wild nature almost anywhere. You can watch the National Geographic channel or subscribe to *Audubon*. You can frequent hiker forums online or become a Facebook fan of a baby bear cub in Minnesota and watch him grow via daily updates. You can read McPhee or Lopez or Ehrlich. I used to find this troubling, the way people waltz into the woods and act as though they're right at home in a place they've never been, when they know nothing of the hardships—the endless drizzle in spring or the inversion in winter or the wildfire smoke in summer—or the tiny miracles either—the first wild currant blooming pink, the shimmer of moonlight on hoarfrost, the cold sweat elation of bucking the last log off the trail and watching it somersault down to the creek. Sitting on my porch with my magazine, I felt more generous. I listened to their laughter rise with road dust through the firs and turned to Shouts & Murmurs.

The invitation to visit the city came, appropriately enough, from a friend I'd never met. In an ironic turn of events, I'd taken a job teaching online for a school based in, yes, New York City. When a student heard that I'd be on the East Coast, in southern Maryland, and might venture north, he offered the use of his Park Slope apartment via email along with a free pass to the Met, a list of walking distance restaurants (thirty of them!), and a subway map. How could I turn down such an offer? I could not. Outwardly I was excited, but inwardly I had concerns. Imagination spurs innovation, sure, and sometimes offers comfort— what is hope, after all, but imagining a better place than where you are?—but it can also be dangerously deceptive.

That very fact had accounted for part of my problem with tourists. Part of my peeve, granted, stemmed from regular don't-pee-on-my-fire-hydrant localism, the kind that makes people buy those godawful bumper stickers— Washington Native, California Native—as if being born in a particular place represents a feat for which you should be congratulated. But part of my unease ran deeper. What *about* that difference between image and reality? If we romanticize wild nature, aren't we ignoring the fact that it's disappearing? Or worse. Aren't we fetishizing it in its decline the way Tolstoy romanticized the yeoman or Michael Pollan extols the glory of the small farmer. Going, going, gone. Ever notice how T-shirt production increases in direct proportion to a species' endangered status? Salmon, wolves, and grizzlies abound on tourist tees. Canada geese? Those once-endangered now ubiquitous city park dwellers? Not so much.

Still, as the bicycle tourists wobbled into view, I knew they saw plenty of reality, sometimes more than I did. Take the deer for instance. I see them every day; sometimes I see them eat my damned flowers. The deer, to me, are pests. I suppose that's how early settlers saw beaver or buffalo or monstrous cedars, how city folks see the geese. Outsiders have a different perspective. The tourists gawk at the dumb-eyed doe that freezes in the middle of the road as a car approaches; they snap photos and exclaim when she stots away, a spotted fawn in her wake. They might be ignorant, these strangers, but at least they are unlikely to decimate whole species. That, if nothing else, is a good thing.

So, my visit to New York. You're thinking, maybe, that things went poorly, that there's no way the city could match my made-up version, but it did. Sort of. Enough. In three days, Laurie and I saw sculptures at MoMA and wept at Strawberry Fields in Central Park—*Imagine* surrounded midwinter by yellow rose petals—and drank mojitos at a restaurant named for my birth city, Bogotá, another three thousand miles away. We didn't attend a book reading or concert but stayed outdoors where, anyway, we are more at home. (My New York, remember, is limned by leaf-filtered sunlight.) But we knew which street names to look for, which to avoid, which direction to go to reach the Village. Were there hardships? Of course. November sleet soaked our light coats and obscured the views. Did I experience poverty or overcrowding or crime or immigrant oppression? Of course not. The visit did not fundamentally change my New York. How could it? What stuck, what sticks, is my own version.

Not long after our return my New York infatuation began to flag. Maybe I gave in to the ridiculousness of the fantasy. When I used to suggest to friends that—who knows?—someday I might move there, they'd double over. You? In New York? They'd choke with laughter. Me in my hem-scraggled work pants and sweat-ringed ball cap? Me with my wide-eyed stare and long-trained propensity to wave at every car that passes? They were right: crazy idea. Then again, maybe the fantasy had worked, giving me the courage to quit my trails job to become a writer and teacher, to swap one tenuous job for another. No, I'm pretty sure the reason I quit going to New York was this: hypocrisy.

The tourists who visit this mountain valley see us the same way they see the deer, as a marvelous novelty. Living the simple life, they think. Just like in the olden days. "What America Was" read belt buckles sold for a while in the local trinket shop. Of course, it's not true. We drive cars and bank online and navigate the complicated world of social connections—family, friends, coworkers—and clashing political beliefs just like anyone else. We watched every episode of *The Wire* one winter and *30 Rock* the next. Even the activities that might make our life seem simple—gardening, canning, wood splitting, skiing to work when the road is unplowed—are anything but. The image is pervasive and sometimes infuriating. You can live up to it or shirk it or try to ignore it until the living up seems intentional or shirking does. (Am I an out lesbian to prove this is not *Little House on the Prairie*?) Is this how people in Manhattan feel? On some level, conscious or subconscious, they must. I remember the shiver I felt the first time I ever heard "Hotel California" as a kid. Even though I lived not a smidge of the glamorous fast-lane life the song describes—we lived in a cul de sac, and besides, I was ten years old—I felt the oppression. Maybe the lifestyle hadn't entrapped me, but I already suspected that the image of being Californian would haunt me my whole life (so far it has), and I wanted to get the hell out. Hence the hypocrisy. We weary of the image of the place we inhabit, so we create ones for other places. Over and over and over.

When I came home from New York that winter, I put on skis and slogged out into soft new snow better than sleet-covered sidewalks any day, yes, better than the city. That's the other argument people make for travel, isn't it? Besides broadening your horizons, sallying forth makes you appreciate home. So, too, with travel in your dreams. When I was a happy kid in California, I pined for the woods. Now I live happily in the woods and conjure the city. Maybe it's restlessness, some hardwired migration instinct not yet snuffed. Or maybe it's something better than that. Something at the core of who we are and who we want to be, a gesture no less startling or poignant for being repeated, like yellow rose petals arranged on icy cement. Imagine. Maybe what helps you stay put is having somewhere you'd rather be.

How to Brine
an Elk Steak

LAST SPRING WHILE RESEARCHING A BOOK, I TOOK A long road trip south to Death Valley hoping to meet with some of the Timbisha Shoshone people, a small tribe that had reclaimed a sliver of their ancestral homeland in a place of seeming scarcity. Along the way, by happenstance and privilege, I ended up staying for a couple of weeks at a writers' retreat in Marin County. I wasn't thinking about food when I set off, but soon it became impossible not to.

Marin County, like many fertile nooks in the region once dubbed Ecotopia, is devoted to food. Land set aside in agricultural trusts supports local dairies, who support local cheese makers, who support local restaurants that serve local wine and organic vegetables. All of it is admirable. It's good for the land, good for the people who own and work the land, and good, too, for the people who sell the food, buy the food, eat the food. I'm telling you, landing in Marin was like landing in Eden, only with no fruit forbidden. At the retreat, we gorged on grass-fed beef, tender arugula, shade-grown coffee, the darkest of chocolates. When I drove down the curvy redwood-lined road, headed for Death Valley, I left behind pungent chèvre and fresh oysters the size of gorilla toes and reentered reality.

Oh, you can try to eat healthy on the road. You can carry a bag of almonds, and when you tire of those, you can stare bleary-eyed at the poster on the fast-food wall that lists all the variables to consider in making your choice: sodium, fiber, protein, calories, fat, cholesterol. You can get a veggie burger at Burger King, fish at Wendy's, a personal pizza at Subway, thick and spongy and white, which is exactly how you feel after seventeen hours in a seat belt. But at some point, it all seems futile.

So you get back in your ancient Buick and scan the radio from preachers to public radio and stumble, inevitably, on a cooking program. Next thing you know, you're taking mental notes on how to brine an elk steak and thinking about your mother, and well, that's when things begin to unravel.

On Monday mornings my mother volunteers at the pantry, which is what they call the food bank at the local parish, Our Lady of Perpetual Help. Maybe they do not call it a "bank" because they don't want to call attention to the fact that the church building looks so much like a bank. Maybe a bank is for saving up, for hoarding, while the pantry is for giving away. Or maybe it's just that "pantry" is a more gentle, homey term with warm kitchen connotations. Mom has gone to the pantry every Monday since she retired from teaching a decade ago except for the year when she was in and out of the hospital with cancer. As soon as she was on her feet, she was back at it.

It's the same drill every Monday. Before she goes to the pantry, she drives to a bakery downtown to collect the day-olds in a Tupperware, then to Starbucks for the same, and finally to a funky new grocery store that caters to individual shoppers, older people, and sells items in plastic wrap—one green pepper and one red one, say, or two zucchinis, or sometimes premade meals, small-sized—where she picks up everything nearing expiration. Then she takes it all to the pantry, to supplement the staples already stored there, and she spends the morning stocking paper bags with peanut butter and tuna, loaves of bread, fruit and vegetables, and an occasional pastry and passes them out to those who wait in line each day, hungry.

Demand at food banks has risen exponentially in recent years, and there is no end in sight. During the week, Mom and her friends shop for the pantry with coupons they clip from the Sunday paper. They watch for deals and drive around town to stock up on staples at the maximum allowable purchase—ten bags of potatoes for a buck, say—or sometimes, on the best days, they use double coupons and walk away with a carload of food and a refund. Each year I send her fifty bucks to spend at the pantry, a modest gift, nearly feeble, and she stretches that fifty thin. She can feed several families for the cost of a round of drinks in the city. It's her version of loaves and fishes, and it leaves me in awe.

Here's the problem: Mom would look askance at Marin. Those cheeses probably cost a pretty penny, she might say. And she'd be right. I wouldn't dare tell her how one day at the grocery store I bought four potatoes, two apples, and a chocolate bar, and my twenty didn't cover the cost.

The question that plagued me as I drove east and then south through blooming almond groves—trees sucking the Central Valley water table dry, in part, to provide almond milk to the non-dairy crowd—the question so obvious that it almost always goes unasked is this: How can you justify paying so much to eat right when so many people can't afford to eat at all? And quick on its heels comes the rebuttal: But what are the costs of not eating right, of abusing the land and our bodies? And why do we always talk about costs anyway, talk as though the earth itself is a bank and not a pantry?

On the road to Death Valley, the cooking program annoyed me, as cooking programs often do. Food talk is everywhere. Click through the channels, surf the Internet, flip through a magazine at the doctor's office, and you'll find recipes for low-fat fettuccine, color photos of pozole with cilantro, growing tips for asparagus. There's food minutia on *The Today Show*, in the local newspaper. Why? Is it pure entertainment? Or is there something missing in our lives, a void we try to fill with food or by denying ourselves food? Or is food the one thing that we can control in a world hurtling toward chaos? We can't solve the Israeli-Palestinian crisis, but we can choose to be vegan or gluten-free. There are plenty of diagnoses and plenty of diets. There are big ideas and big words: egalitarianism vs. localism, fairness vs. righteousness, psychology vs. physiology. Mostly there is talk.

The talk on this program, as I've said, was about how to brine an elk steak, and that too annoyed me because recently we'd had an elk steak we got wrong. This steak—the kind of clean lean red meat that would cost a small fortune at Whole Foods—was a gift to us, or more specifically to Laurie, who maintains a historic apple orchard. Each winter, around the full moon of February, a herd of elk visits the orchard to stand on the hard crust of snow and eat bark off the trees. They are lovely animals, yes, regal, majestic even, but Laurie, on balance, cares more about the trees. She's eager for local hunters to get lucky, but they rarely do since hunting season is November, not February, and the elk are wily besides.

One day when we stopped to pick up milk from neighbors who keep a cow, there it was, a single steak wrapped in butcher paper and labeled with a Sharpie: "Apple-fed. Merry Christmas." We took it home and fried it in a pan, and even though it was the best Christmas gift Laurie received, even though it was the best meat I've ever had in my life, we could have done better. Panfried? Really? When, on the road to Death Valley, I heard about that brine on the radio, I knew, that would've been the way. That slow brine would've been an act of honor, of gratitude for our hunter-neighbor, for the elk, for the apple trees that fed them.

I pulled over to jot down the recipe gist, then switched the radio off and continued in silence, crawling through notches in gray granite mountains, tire tracks in slush swerving around windblown pine limbs, then pines giving way to juniper giving way to Joshua trees, until nothing was left but cloud shadows on alluvial fans.

Before heading into the park, I stopped at a Nevada mini-mart and scoured the shelves for something, anything, healthy to eat, but after a few minutes I gave up. Label reading at a gas station with the smell of stale cigarettes in the air and the jangle of slot machines in the background seemed somehow wrong. Pretentious. So I grabbed Fritos and bean dip and headed for camp. By sunset, I sat alone and content on hot sand by my tent watching sunlight illuminate lime-green mesquite blossoms, scraping the hot metal can with the Frito edge, and thinking about the Timbisha Shoshone.

The original inhabitants of Death Valley survived on pinion nuts and mesquite beans, bighorn sheep and quail.

They focused no less on food than we do, but they were closer to it. They watched blossoms migrate from desert to mountains, and come fall, they followed the harvest the other way. They ground the seeds and saved the paste and remembered the old ways; they do it still. Traditional Ecological Knowledge, the anthropologists call it, TEK, and it's about more than food. It's knowing the plants and animals that surround you and how to use them in ways that do not deplete and do not harm and passing that knowledge on through generations, not as a technical feat or a profitable enterprise, but as culture itself.

After dinner, I walked a windblown ridge, feeling not quite hungry but not quite right, thinking about the people who'd line up in the morning at the pantry and the dairy farmers who'd wake at dawn and how we're all connected, in the end, by long freeway miles and radio airwaves, by rainfall and drought and elected leaders. In the fading light, the desert landscape appeared stark and empty, as though it could not possibly produce enough food to go around.

But it did. For centuries, it did.

In the morning, I joined a small gathering of Timbisha Shoshone at a table outside an adobe home in Furnace Creek and listened to elders talk about how the miners and government tried for decades to run them off as well as the pressures of gaming, corruption in the Bureau of Indian Affairs, and unemployment that at times runs as high as 80 to 90 percent. Even though they've survived for centuries and even though they fought and won a battle to reclaim land from no less than the government of the United States of America, sometimes it must seem like the situation cannot possibly improve. Do they ever feel like giving up? I asked.

"It's easy to feel like giving up," one elder said. She gazed up toward the place near a natural spring where her people once lived, the place where an inn now sits that charges $400 a night. Sand blew against pickup trucks. Mourning doves called. From behind us, in the house, canned laughter blared from a television. She turned to face me.

"But it is very hard to give up."

Her expression remained unreadable, but her message felt clear. Neither boast nor encouragement, it felt like admonishment. The core principle of TEK, after all, isn't sustainability; it's resiliency.

As noon approached, grandchildren emerged from the house and served us bologna sandwiches with potato chips and cold water in plastic cups. The first bite transported me instantly to my childhood, when bologna, like liverwurst and chocolate milk, was healthy for kids, and I felt overcome with sadness, near outrage, at the injustice caused by unthinking privilege. We tell ourselves times have changed, and we know better. We tell ourselves we can make right what's gone wrong, but it's complicated. It's not just what we eat, but how we live. Not just what you grow or hunt or choose to buy, but what you endure, what you sacrifice, and, ultimately, what you share.

There were many miles left, for me. Three more Buick breakdowns. Several more snowy passes. More veggie burgers and french fries, smushy store-bought apples, and once, just once, a can of Red Bull. Later at home, we'd return to doing the best we knew how. We'd plant Swiss chard and tomatoes, buy lamb from a friend and whole-grain bread from the bakery. We'd bring the best stuff to potlucks or save it for company, and each year we'd send money to Mom for the pantry.

Meanwhile, in Furnace Creek, I took one last bite of bread crust and drained the last of my water and thanked my hosts. No food, the entire trip, will have been so nourishing.

Post-Strayed

EACH SUMMER WHILE WE MOVED HEAVY ROCKS OR SAWED suspended logs or cleared head-high stinging nettles, Pacific Crest Trail thru-hikers, those heading to Canada from Mexico, sped past us. They needed to keep moving because they were so close to the end—only eighty miles shy of the border, they were, in some ways, sick of it all—and because they usually wore shorts despite thick swarms of biting black flies. Those of us who had to actually work, to stand amid the onslaught, kept every inch of skin clothed.

Back in town, after work, we'd run into the thru-hikers, scruffy and unshowered, in the post office as they collected the resupply boxes they'd sent ahead to themselves. Many were hiking alone, so they were desperate to talk to someone, to anyone, and you could get stuck for way too long if you weren't careful. Some neighbors griped about that or about the body odor stench, but neither the chatter nor the smell bugged me much. The attitude did. They acted proud, exceedingly so, and entitled to the random kindnesses bestowed on them over months on the trail, the gifts from trail angels: food, rides, a bed or a shower, sometimes cash. The hikers gushed dreamily about the miracle of it all, like ticket-grubbing stoners outside Grateful Dead concerts.

Over beer around a campfire, we sneered freely. How privileged were these modern-day pilgrims with quadriceps thick as hams who prattled on and on, frantic and breathless? Who could afford to take an entire summer off to walk? The truth was any of us could. We were used to frugality but wouldn't allow ourselves the frivolity. We believed in hard work and in loyalty to one place.

I sometimes joked that when thru-hikers bragged about hiking twenty-five hundred miles, we should say we'd hiked just as many PCT miles, but all on the same fifteen-mile stretch, one on which we knew every marshy bog, every sun-scorched switchback, every patch of boxwood or wild cherry. We knew where to find long-stashed rock bars, usable outhouses, peek-a-views of peaks, where you were likely to encounter a bear or a porcupine. We knew the trail, as they say, like the backs of our hands or our hard-calloused palms.

Of course, we said no such thing to thru-hikers. We didn't say much at all. We listened politely, congratulated them, and got back to work. These were our customers, after all, more like our employers since their taxes paid our wages, and we were glad, genuinely, to see the trails getting use. Underneath it all, we believed we were the real thing, and they were not.

Over time Laurie and I offered thru-hikers grudging respect—it *is* a long way to walk—and occasional kindnesses: a two-pound block of cheddar for the woman with a llama subsisting on edible plants; a ride in the back of our pickup for the woman with her small son, the youngest ever to complete the trail, a blind eye for the guy camping illegally since he was hiking with two very large trunks (rumored to be packed with bars of soap) that he hauled across fifty-yard stretches, one at a time. We gave away socks and bags of chocolate, beer on occasion, and once an old pair of running shoes. We didn't go as far as others. No camping in the yard. No free meals or showers. If you start that business, within days word would be out. Everyone would knock on your door.

All of this was before *Wild*.

As soon as I heard about the memoir, I recalled the first time I'd heard about the movie *Titanic*. What a silly idea, I'd thought. That's the oldest story in the book. The memory came charging back like a cautionary tale. The Pacific Crest Trail? Everyone knew that story, didn't they? Then I thought again. I'd read Cheryl Strayed's essays and admired them, and I had an inkling *Wild* would be a good book. And it was, excellent in fact, a book about an inner journey through grief and into selfhood. I loved the way the trail grounded the story, kept it moving, and the way Strayed portrayed herself too: never the braggart, never the victim, raw, vulnerable, smart, unapologetic, sad and lonely, but resilient as hell. The lyric prose moved steady and sturdy, clear, rhythmic, and right. More than anything, the story seemed true, like what this woman truly needed to say. Not what she needed to say about hiking, but what she needed to say about life, truth, beauty, love.

I figured that was all I had to say about *Wild*. But I was wrong. The book haunted me. People who read the memoir—friends, neighbors, coworkers, students, sometimes strangers on the ferry—asked me about it. At first, I'd happily engage. I'd explain what I admired, but clearly my enthusiasm disappointed people. They wanted me to scoff, or better yet, to tear into Cheryl Strayed.

Some readers disapproved of Strayed's promiscuity on the trail, which made me wonder, What else did they read? Did they never watch HBO? Had they never sown oats themselves in their twenties? None? I didn't want to know, so I held my tongue. Others struggled with her characterization of heroin use. People who'd faced addiction, personally or with friends or family, could not abide her casual use or her easy abandonment of the drug. To them I had no reply. I couldn't say whether someone could toy with heroin then drop it. I could say only that Strayed did not strike me as a liar.

Outdoorsy types took issue with her unpreparedness. Backpacking, after all, depends on careful planning. The sheer number of gadgets and tricks to reduce pack weight constitutes a regular OCD candy shop. Even if you lean sloppy, as I always had, it takes time and intention, as well as cash and ingenuity, to learn what you need to carry, what you don't, and it takes time and commitment to get in shape for a long trek. Strayed, they said, hadn't even tried. I tried to mention how often we saw unprepared hikers in the woods—every single day—and how none of them died. If they suffered, they brought home a good story. Just like Strayed did.

Finally, people bristled at the fact that she didn't finish the trail. She hiked 1,100 of 2,650 miles. It didn't seem to matter that she never intended to finish or that maybe not finishing made her more human and relatable to readers who aren't hard-core hikers. This one was easiest to dismiss. I'd heard the same complaints about Bill Bryson's *A Walk in the Woods*. Not prepared? Check. Not in shape? Check. Not enough knowledge about the trail? Check. He walked only 870 miles out of 2,200 on the Appalachian Trail. Plus he had outright complaints, way more than Strayed. All those damned trees: boring, boring, boring. I tried to remind Strayed's detractors about Bryson, but people shook their heads in disgust. Some seethed.

After a while, I desperately wanted to avoid conversations about *Wild*. But I couldn't. I had to keep defending the book because, well, this was madness. Misogyny seemed to lie at the heart of it. Do we demand such authenticity of men? I never saw "I hate Bill Bryson" blogs, but type "I hate Cheryl Strayed" into a search engine and you'll find plenty, and the sheer viciousness reminded me of attacks against Hillary Clinton, the near-apoplectic sense of outrage. I hadn't heard it this bad since *Eat, Pray, Love*. (I'd later learn Strayed and Elizabeth Gilbert faced similar challenges with similar grace. Individually, they kept urging women to speak and write honestly. Together, they raised money for Syrian refugees.) As with Clinton and Gilbert, much of the venom came from women. Over and over they asked the same question: What has Cheryl Strayed done that's so much better than me?

I'd be lying if I said I'd never thought it myself. When *Wild* came out, I'd already written a book about working on trails that sold many million copies fewer than Strayed's. If I thought too hard about that fact, envy crept in cloaked in deservedness. I spent fifteen years on the trails, and she spent three months. I had committed myself genuinely and was not passing "thru" casually. Part of me wanted to believe I had earned the right to write.

But I'd already fought that demon and lost. The idea that you must commit your life to authentic living before you write about it is patent bullshit. Melville signed up for four years on a whaling ship but deserted on the Marquesas Islands after eighteen months as an ordinary seaman. Samuel Clemens was a steamboat pilot for four years before the Civil War intruded—thankfully for all of us who cherish Twain's books—and he had to give it up. Four years proved long enough for him to conjure a misty night of snags and shifting sandbars. Even the shortest experience has vivid and lasting influence. One summer my eight-year-old niece and I went on a memorable hike at dawn, about which she wrote an illustrated account, "The Abandoned Trail." In the corner, she added her own nod to authenticity: "This relly happened!"

What I mean to say, what took me a damned long time to learn, is this: You don't need years of experience to earn the right to write. In fact, when you spend all your time, say, hiking, what you get good at is hiking. Cheryl Strayed spent three months hiking, then she spent years honing the craft of writing, putting it before every other aspect of her life, going into credit card debt. You don't have to read the many interviews where she says so outright to know this about Cheryl Strayed. Read "The Love of My Life," as searing an essay as exists in English. Read *Torch*, a gorgeous novel about hard grief. *Wild* isn't an anomaly, it's a culmination. Strayed's motto isn't "hike like a motherfucker," it's "write like a motherfucker."

I didn't say all that to every detractor, but I did say this: she wrote a beautiful book. Even when people sidled up to me to suggest she had a better agent, sold out her writing style to suit Hollywood, or got lucky with Oprah, I told them in no uncertain terms: None of that changes the truth. She wrote a beautiful book.

So it was that I'd been defending Strayed for more than a year when I headed to Boston for a writing conference. I'd never been to the city and rarely to the East Coast. I bought clothes and shoes, not for the weather but to play pseudo-professional woman or at least not-in-Levi's woman. The convention center had been designed, as I suppose convention centers always are, so we never had to walk outside. Desperate, I found ways around it and ruined my city shoes walking in snowmelt gutters, past wily panhandlers, alone in the dark, just to watch snow swirl in the streetlights and to smell the wind off the river. I stopped to eat cheap sushi in a window seat watching hunched pedestrians in overcoats hustle past on the sidewalk and then I headed back to the convention center.

One reception, then another. Two glasses of wine later, I arrived in a room packed to the hilt to watch Cheryl Strayed walk onstage in a bright red dress, tight around her hips, with deep cleavage showing. She sat, crossed her legs, and smiled lipstick large. I don't remember what she said, though I am sure she was kind and thoughtful, earnest and edgy at once, the Dear Sugar persona, though we hadn't yet met Sugar. So I had no excuse, except perhaps the wine, when I was utterly blindsided.

I began to weep, and then sob, alone in the auditorium crowd, snot-faced without tissues. What on earth was my problem? The dress for starters. When I saw her in the red dress, I felt exactly like I do when I go into a dressing room at the mall, like something is expected of me that I am not quite capable of. My near-constant uniform, a plaid shirt and blue jeans, the exact same clothes I wore as a child and what I wear now, may be authentic woods-wear, but it's not marketable author-wear. I'd spent years writing about how, on trail crew, I was never quite man enough, but here in the convention center, I suddenly felt not woman enough.

I stood and left. I longed for the windblown snow, and the walk back to the hotel calmed me and made me realize that what hurt most was not the highly marketable femininity, nor the fact—shameful to admit it even occurred to me—that Strayed was not terribly physically fit, not even the accumulated exasperation of months of defending one good book when I read a whole lot of them. Her persona onstage made one thing clear. She achieved success because she wanted it, and she was unafraid to make it happen. She had ambition, and I told myself I did not. Or not enough. I could buy shoes, fly across the continent, give presentations on the craft of writing, even publish books steadily, one after the next. None of it was enough. Cheryl Strayed was the real thing, and I was not.

Land managers estimate that before 2012 when *Wild* appeared, three hundred people used to thru-hike the PCT in a year. In 2016 I heard nearly three thousand, which is odd considering the other trails on our district, miles and miles of them, remain well-maintained and virtually unused. Of course, on those trails no one gives you free stuff. You won't get a special trail name, but you're more likely to find solitude. The trailhead may be harder to reach, but the views will undoubtedly be better.

If the view from our post office is any indication, a ten-fold increase on the PCT seems about right. On any given summer day, the postmaster stands behind a wall of boxes larger than during Christmas week and longer, too, since this onslaught will last through October. If I want to buy stamps, I'm going to have to wait. The hikers crowd the porch steps of the post office, tearing open the familiar white priority mail boxes greedily, tossing packaging in the bear-proof garbage cans, and sorting through baggies of pasta and jerky, fistfuls of energy bars and Snickers, leaving excess in a communal take-it-or-leave-it box that is heavy on quick oats and dried milk. They know now, better than when they started, what they want. No use carrying anything extraneous.

One thing walking the PCT requires is ambition, not to *be* something but to *do* something, to achieve a named thing, an observable thing. Maybe that's why the rest of the trails go untraveled. Solitude is not the goal. Nor are superlative views. Achievement is. On trail crew, we carried heavy packs. We slept soaked and sweated hard. On days so hot firefighters were told to hunker in the shade, we still worked. Was it an achievement? Not really. It was a job; it was regular life. Self-awareness, I suppose, takes longer than 1,100 miles or 2,650. You can be changed on a long trail, true. You can be changed on the subway or in a lounge chair with the right book, changed by changing diapers, changed by chopping through a buried root thick as your forearm, digging a signpost hole with a chainsaw wrench, sleeping in a wet sleeping bag or a crappy motel, but usually you are not changed by regular life.

On my way home from Boston, a wave of gratitude wholly unexpected and near-cliché washed over me as we flew over the winter-white Rockies and then the Cascades. So many memories: yellow light warm on velvet heather in spring, huckleberries red as flames cloaked in the first snow of fall, the sweet smell of creosote on bridge timbers, the cedar soft tread underfoot in the forest, the roar of charging snowmelt close while you tighten splintery deck boards to three-eighths cable over the froth, and then finally, glaciers wedged in granite against blue sky as far as you can see, views boot-earned better than the ones from a window seat can ever be. I was wrong to believe I lacked ambition. For many years, more than anything else, I wanted to be *out there*, bugs and bears and heat and heaving breath and over-fast heart rate and all.

So I approach the old demon again, humble and insistent. I didn't hike so I could write about it. I hiked because I love to hike. People say ambition comes from the heart, but I'm not convinced. Ambition follows your body, and your body follows your ambition. That's what people hate about Cheryl Strayed and Hillary Clinton. Ditto for the swarms of PCT hikers, more and more of whom are women. It's not jealousy of success so much as the near-outrage we feel toward anyone who knows, even for a short time, exactly what she wants and turns herself, as they say, body and soul to the task.

Last weekend my teenaged nephews showed up. City kids in decent shape but not mountain climbers by any stretch. They wanted to go up McGregor Mountain, sixteen miles round-trip, eight thousand feet elevation gain. I'd planned to spend the day writing, but the sky promised to be clear, the temperature perfect, the views stunning. So we went, boots scuffing on gravel and retinas burning from sun reflecting off snow. We made it to the top, came home with muscles like mush, too exhausted to read, much less to write. On the way back down the dirt road from the trailhead in our pickup, we passed a group of PCT hikers, sweaty in the road dust and heading for the post office. You could tell they wouldn't mind a ride, but they didn't bother to hold out a thumb. So we passed them by.

Away from Shore

AS A KID, I SWAM ALL SUMMER IN BACKYARD POOLS AND at the city park. Lessons in the morning, wildness all afternoon. My bare feet grew calluses, my hair turned brittle green, my shoulders got broad. In high school, I raced butterfly and breaststroke and returned home fit and famished to devour plates of fettuccine made with whole cream. In college: laps before dawn in the basement of an ivy-walled hall, followed by the morning's first lecture, hair wet, and a clean notebook page. Then, in my early twenties, I moved to the woods.

There's no pool here, no pool for miles. There is a beautiful lake, gorgeous, narrow, and long, cupped by rocky ridges like prayerful hands or the sides of a canoe. It's a natural lake, carved a millennia ago by the long tongue of a glacier and raised twenty feet by a dam in the twenties. Even without the dam, it's a deep lake, the third deepest in North America behind Crater Lake and Lake Tahoe, as you'll hear via narration on the ferry, the *Lady of the Lake*, every single time you ride. It's an astonishing shifting color: popsicle-blue or steamed spinach green or sometimes, in winter, on a cloud-dark day, an oily, ominous black. In summer, wind-whipped waves rimmed with sunlit glare move downlake in orderly formation as dry heat from the Columbia River draws cool air from the still snowy peaks—the lake is fed by twenty-seven glaciers. So, it's gorgeous, yes, but it's also very cold.

Leap from the dock on the hottest day of August, and you'll emerge sputtering for air. You can't stay in five minutes. Sometimes you can't stay at all. At the Chelan end of the lake, fifty-five miles from here, it's not nearly as bad, sixty degrees or even seventy, cool and refreshing. But at our end, closer to the mouth of the river, it can be twenty degrees cooler. Sometimes, often, I used to gaze out at the unswimmable expanse with abject longing. If only. If only.

Onshore, neighbors gather with inflatable toys and coolers of cold drinks, watermelon slices and half-soggy magazines. Kids somehow manage to stay in the frigid water longer, wading waist-deep, lining up like mergansers on the mossy logs, standing or sitting, sometimes shivering. Some neighbors, because of religion, don't show skin; they splash about in dresses or jeans. Others don't get wet at all but loll on the grass tossing sticks for dogs. The scene is inclusive, laid-back, and sometimes claustrophobic.

This is the small-town problem. You know everyone, and they know you. Even though they're people you love—many of them, most of them—sometimes you want to get away. For that, you have miles, *thousands* of miles, of wilderness, but August in the backcountry is hot and dusty and buggy—so thick with flies, you can't expose an inch of DEET-free skin—and sometimes you're feeling too lazy to carry a pack. So, back to the lake.

I tried windsurfing for a few years—pulling up the sail over and over and falling in the water. I wore a child-sized Spider-Man wetsuit for which I'd traded a raincoat. It'd work fine for twenty minutes or so, as long as I was mostly standing on the board, not submerged, dragging the whole rig—mast, sailboard, and all—back to the dock against the wind, as I so often was. Meanwhile, a few neighbors had begun to swim seriously, the schoolteacher for one. They bought better wetsuits and swam in scuba hoods with booties. I talked to them shyly about their gear and even got a hood and booties of my own. I'd swim a few hundred yards, but I was too cold. I'd climb out and shiver. Even with a down coat, even with the heater on full blast in the car for the drive home, even as I stood in the shower, draining the hot water tank, still I'd shiver.

I'd fantasized about open-water swimming plenty over the years, mostly because of Lynne Cox, whose memoir,

Swimming to Antarctica, chronicles how she swam from a California beach to Catalina Island—twenty-one miles of open water—when she was fourteen years old, how she swam the Nile with dead rats floating around her, how she swam from Chile to Antarctica in water viscous with ice, and how she swam the Bering Strait from Alaska to Russia. She describes her Bering Strait swim as a peace mission of sorts, one that ended up facilitating dialogue between Gorbachev and Reagan. I loved her stories. I was awed by the power of this decidedly non-celebrity super-endurance athlete swimming to make a difference, and without a wetsuit no less. I talked about her so much that one cold fall morning when I was slow to crawl out of my tent, my crewmates teased me that Lynne Cox would not be in bed.

But I am no Lynne Cox. For one thing, I am more prone to panic than I like to admit. I have little of the mountain climber's can-do or the addict's fuck-you. Once, years ago, some friends and I made the foolish choice to swim across the lake on a whim without wetsuits. We did OK owing to one-hundred-degree weather until we reached the mouth of the river where the water temperature drops precipitously. Swimming out front, I raised my head to holler, "I'm cramping up! I'm cramping up!" A friend flailing behind me yelled back, "You're ten feet from shore."

I'd all but given up when, one summer, a friend persuaded me to sign up for a triathlon. It didn't seem like too big a stretch. For years I'd been paid to hike for exercise; now I jogged regularly, if not strenuously, and I'd always ridden a bike for transportation. I could ramp up my running mileage and ride my bike in laps up and down four short miles of pavement. The challenge would be the swim. No way around it, I'd have to train in the lake. After all those years, that's all it took. I bought a new wetsuit, thick and buoyant and made for movement.

Suddenly, I could stay in.

In open water, distance is hard to gauge. Midlake, a long log—gray, weathered, and creased like skin—juts at a narrow angle just above the water. Farther out, another lies flat and mossy green with tufts of grass atop; seagulls line it like a brigade. Farther on, a crisscrossed jumble lies close to where the icy river water seeps in. For a while I swam each day to the first log to rest and then swam back to shore. Later, as I grew stronger, I swam from one log to the next, then the next. I swam around a grassy island, past nesting geese and a kids' hidden fort. I swam and swam and swam.

To swim is to sever ties. Without goggles, you can't see much. Far from shore, you can't stand up. Without surfacing, you can't even breathe. The only sound I could hear was a boat's motor revving. If the surface is still, those on the shore could hear my kicking feet splash. If I was breathing hard, they could hear me exhale. But I could never hear them. Even without the scuba hood, I was in my own world. I craved it. I reveled in it. There had always been plenty of reasons to swim—fitness, camaraderie, mental alertness, plain glee—but my most vivid memories remained underwater, soundless and weightless and utterly alone. The opening sequence of *The Graduate* makes me ache. Underwater you're like the kid at a dinner party, nose in a book, in the middle of the fray, with the hubbub of humans, the too-loud laughter, the booze and cigarettes, and the mess of chip crumbs on the coffee table. You can be there and not, all at once. Records show humans have been swimming for a very long time. The Cave of Swimmers in Egypt dates back ten thousand years, a pool in India five thousand. Characters swim in the *Iliad*, the *Odyssey*, the Bible. But why? Sure, people swam of necessity, to get from here to there. But maybe they also swam to get away.

When people ask why I ever moved to such an isolated place, I clench and turn inward, defensive, wanting to explain that I'm not an oddball, not at all, that it was the vagaries of circumstance, a coincidence like any other. But it's not true. Of course, I came here to get away. People used to accuse Laurie and me of this early on when we were first coming out. No roads? No phones even? Way to hide! We denied it, even as we wondered if our love could've survived anywhere else. But my urge to get away predates us, though I can't, even now, precisely define what I needed to get away from. Away from family tension? Mine was no worse than some families' and better by a mile than others. Away from a world of trouble? The world was less troubled in 1989, you could argue, than at most other times last century, and way better than now. Away from the sheer commotion of modern life? That strikes closer to home. I loved acoustic instruments, moldy paperbacks, cast-iron cookware, anything out of fashion or step. As a new adult, I hiked and backpacked alone a lot. I took road trips and slept in rest stops, taking astonishing risks, I now think, for a nineteen-year-old girl, but it wasn't the danger that attracted me any more than it's the danger in the water. I wanted to be out of step. I wanted to put space between myself and almost everything, and the perspective from this remote valley, especially after a long trip, sometimes feels precisely as exhilarating as looking back at shore from the middle of the lake.

With goggles, you see everything: submerged logs, rocks on the bottom, swaying aquatic grasses, more rarely a fish or a snake. Most life hovers above. Swallows diving for insects, plus seagulls and ospreys and eagles diving for fish. Sometimes when I turned my head and hips to breathe, I held that pose hoping to watch one dive, but it hardly ever happened. Instead, I'd watch my hand reenter the water, cross the wavery surface, then reach forward as I rolled facedown. Fingers held tight, hand slightly bent in parade-wave pose, I pulled in toward my belly and then out toward my hip, in a curve more S than C, trying to maximize propulsion. Sometimes I'd look down through clear water and see a large peace symbol, fifteen or twenty feet across, made of river rocks set in the sand by short-term neighbors one winter when the lake was drawn down. The neighbors were long gone, but the peace symbol remained. I always tried to find it, and sometimes I couldn't. When I did, it felt like a good omen. When I climbed out, I felt remade. Every time.

I've always admired the way a swimmer looks like a marionette who's been lifted by strings to stand tall. Watching my young nieces, who swim on a team in a New Jersey lake, walk across a dock to the starting blocks takes my breath away. Those high shoulders, those narrow hips. Lynne Cox looks nothing like that. She's short and heavy, layers of protection for her heart in the coldest of cold. Researchers have studied her metabolism to try to understand its ability to withstand cold. Her body temperature, they've found, actually rises the colder she gets, as though she's not just adapted to swimming in cold water but is made for it.

All of Lynne Cox's feats impress me, but Catalina stands out. For a week each year when I was young, my family headed to the beach, and we kids stayed in the water for hours. (The only rule was you had to get out when you started to shiver. *I'm not fridgering*! I'd insist, lips blue and quivering. *I'm not!*) I stood waist-deep in the churn, watching ripples of sunlight move toward me on the waves, the waves, diving under them, jumping over them, then standing again to watch for Catalina. The island hovered on the horizon, visible at times and invisible more often than not in haze or clouds. Every time it emerged, we announced it with the same glee as when we spied a pod of dolphins. *Look: there's Catalina!*

I returned to the book not long ago and realized I'd forgotten a key point. Lynne Cox didn't train alone. She trained to swim to Catalina Island with a group of teenagers, and they planned to make the journey together, but when the day came, some in the group struggled mightily. Coaches and others urged Lynne to forge ahead—she had a decent chance to break the world record—but she refused, even though she got colder treading water, even though the longer she waited, the greater the chance she wouldn't make it at all. Even when the two fastest guys passed her by to forge ahead, she waited for the last swimmer. They swam to safety together.

At the triathlon, a group of friends I'd met other places, outside the mountain valley in the away-from-home life I'd begun to nurture, gathered. We hopped barefooted on gravel trying to stay warm, trying to avert nerves, while instructions boomed out through a bullhorn. At last, we waded in to tread water, grouped by age and gender and swim cap color. The water temperature hovered in the low seventies. I didn't need a wetsuit, but I wore one anyway. For buoyancy. For security. Trees swayed on the lakeshore. Spectators loitered. A horn blasted, and swimmers took off in mad splashing fury. Unless I raised my head, I could not see other bodies, but I could feel them, the roil of movement, the kicking especially, and more than once I bumped straight into them, so I lifted my head again to see the orange buoy marking the turnaround, and took a long outside detour around the bodies. If it slowed me down, so be it. Until the homestretch, when there was no choice. I swerved back inward, toward the finish, and rejoined the churn, exhilarated to be swimming alone, together, all of us.

Back home, as summer waned, I sometimes swam with others. One evening we swam away from a campfire party at dusk while dogs barked on the roadside, an osprey perched atop a snag, flocks of gulls circled like swifts, wide white shrouds against granite, then spiraled out of view. One Sunday, we swam across the lake, nearly a mile, with paddleboard escorts. We swam, unwittingly, with our arms in perfect sync, like marchers in a parade, like birds in flight. We reached the far shore and rested on a smooth slab of rock beneath Indian pictographs painted centuries before. Then we turned for home, no longer in perfect sync, finding our own separate courses, but in the same cold water, in it together.

Only once did I get into trouble. Late in the season, even with all the gear—wetsuit, booties, gloves, hood, goggles—my face hit the water and the sting came as a shock. I told myself, Keep swimming, you'll get used to it. I stopped at the first log to catch my breath and take in the view: yellow alders on the hillsides, red vine maples in steep chutes, blue sky bluer than summer, bluer than anything, and the lake reflecting it all. It was beautiful, yes, stunning. But it hurt more each time I put my face back in. I swam hard to stay warm, confident with late season strength, past the grassy island to the second log. Not more than a quarter mile out, I turned to breathe and felt my chest squeeze and reminded myself that it was just asthma reacting to the cold. ("You're ten feet from shore!") I turned on my back to wheeze (my chest tightens as I write) and tore at my scuba hood too tight around my neck, too tight against my windpipe. I pulled off a glove to get a better grip on the neoprene, but I couldn't get the hood off. I could see a familiar pickup passing on the road, and I waved wildly to drivers who happily waved back, and I remembered my high school English textbook, with a poem by Stevie Smith "I'm not waving but drowning," and how melodramatic it felt even then and how true. I waved and waved until I had no choice but to swim back, rolling over occasionally to wheeze, watching tourists walk with baggies of bread from the bakery swinging by their sides. I could've called to them then, but by then I knew I was OK. I'd make it just fine. Back onshore, gasping while I dried myself, I watched an osprey flying fast, fish in her talons facing backward, by instinct or design, for aerodynamic efficiency.

When Lynne Cox swam to Antarctica, she swam among chunks of ice "like upside down sno-cones" and toward penguins sliding down ice. She swam 1.06 miles in thirty-two-degree water. She was forty-six years old. Two years later, Lynne Cox faced a health scare. I was shocked by the news. If anyone seemed immortal to me, it was Lynne Cox. She recounts the story in a newer memoir *Swimming in the Sink*. Doctors told her she'd need a heart transplant, and she refused. Instead, she reconsidered her diet, her habits, her relationships, and changed what she could. Eventually, miraculously, she recovered by moving her arms through ice water, as though the cold steadied her heart. The solution to her troubles, it turned out, was twofold: to take the time to shift her perspective and then return to what she'd always done, who she'd always been.

And so we swim. Submerge, arise gasping, submerge again, until the rhythm smooths. Stroke, breathe, stroke, breathe. There's this moment when you turn, arm outstretched, and the water surface splits the world in two, safety above and danger below. On the horizon, mountains rise and reflect while underwater your hand pulls down and away, moving you through the cold, farther and farther from shore, until you touch the mossy log—an arbitrary destination—and turn back toward home.

The Tree in the River

THE TREE STANDS IN THE MIDDLE OF THE RIVER, NOT IN
a shallow side channel, but smack in the middle of the
current. Barkless, the trunk battered and discolored like
a splotchy ill patient or worse—technically the tree is a
snag—but still it stands, a hundred feet tall or more, with
limbs that elbow toward the sky. The tree used to stand on
dry ground, of course, a massive Ponderosa, orange-barked
and majestic, beside a horse trail through the woods. When
a major flood came to our valley years ago, the river broad-
ened and chiseled away at the bank, claiming the entire
trail and a large chunk of road to boot.

We never saw it coming. We should've seen it coming. One-hundred-year floods had wreaked havoc before

but nothing like this. This time, entire swaths of forest dropped into the drink, roots and all, like rolling up sod to move elsewhere. I sometimes try to picture the trail that once skirted the tree, a trail on which tourists rode docile, sure-footed horses twice a day over a small creek on a wooden bridge. Each fall we'd clear accumulated dirt and duff from the decking, pushing it through the cracks, trying to keep rot at bay. Rot. As if. The bridge disappeared in the flood, washed away until all that remained were chunks of cedar decking strewn and silt-coated in the woods.

But the tree still stands. We pass by in a car or on bikes or, most often, on skis. The rerouted road isn't plowed that far, so we cross-country ski past the tree regularly, and every time we do, we stop by the place in the river where it stands, to sip water or to peel off a layer, and mostly to marvel. The tree is still there!

For years, another bridge, North Fork, farther in the backcountry, along the Pacific Crest Trail, took more of our attention. We never knew when we'd take the once-a-year trek to shovel off the snow. Seven miles on skis to a cabin, three more the next morning to the bridge, a few hours of shoveling and then either back to the cabin or home. One overnight if you hustled, two if you had sense. Either way the trip required planning. You'd have to go when schedules allowed, when storms didn't threaten, when snow had not hardened to treacherous ice.

North Fork Bridge was built in 1950, a wooden truss bridge with an eighty-foot span. Trail crew began shoveling in the early seventies. By the time I started in the nineties, the bridge was almost historic—a designation that only comes after fifty years—and in heavy winters, snow accumulated impressively, piling high and curling over the upper trusses like a well-risen loaf of bread. How much would be enough to weaken the bridge irrevocably, to stress the trusses or crush them? We didn't know. We weren't engineers—"specs" and "tolerances" not part of our vocabulary—but shoveling couldn't hurt. Then again, maybe it could. Government money only gets allocated when a bridge collapses. Maybe we should've let it go. But we couldn't. Tradition and ambition goaded us on and a kind of old-timey challenge too—"to earn our Girl Scout badges," Laurie called it—plus the beauty of the silent woods in winter and the near-desperate need to get the hell out from under the eternal inversions—cold air trapped low, soupy with woodsmoke—and into the backcountry.

In early years we followed the unplowed road, wide and steady and nearly flat, easy to ski. Easy most years, I should say. Some years, giant ice cones formed along the road cuts, high round knobs you had to clamber over herringbone style, and sometimes mist from the river rose and settled on the cones and then froze hard like a candied apple glaze that a metal ski edge couldn't nick much less edge. If you slipped, you'd slide into the river and almost surely die. We did not want to die, so if the cones got big enough, the conditions icy enough, we'd take the trail instead. And that required following markers; some were hand-painted with skiers and many just tin can lids we'd spray-painted orange and nailed high on a tree, ten feet or twelve. Even if you'd walked the trail a hundred times before and skied it dozens, without those markers you'd be lost.

Now, after the flood, the road had washed away entirely, so the trail remained the only option. Meanwhile, on the crew, longtime employees had left or quit, retired or died. A group of friends volunteered to shovel the bridge, but they had never been on a winter trek to North Fork Bridge. I knew the way, so did Laurie. But I was no longer employed, and while I'd happily volunteer, we had a cat to consider. Daisy was old and sick, rarely eating and only drinking when lifted to the faucet. We figured only one of us needed to go all the way to North Fork. The other would stay with the cat. Since I had some desk work—who knows what? nothing crucial in hindsight—I'd stay home, but since Laurie had to work at the orchard in the morning, and could ski plenty fast enough to catch up, we decided I'd lead the new crew up the trail.

We followed the tin-can-top markers affixed, barely visible, to darkened trunks—fir, cedar, pine, and many draped with lichen like tinsel. It was cold but not too cold, snowing but not hard. Even breaking trail took less effort than usual. Normally, even on the best day, the second person in line needs to do some work. At worst, everyone ends up breaking through snow as it refills the track, like grain in a silo, or snow sticks to the waxless ski base like thick slabs of sheet cake, and you get overheated but you never stop, because if you stop, you'll get too cold, so you keep moving. Normally you'd have to plod upstream among thick branches and brambles, over downed logs and around boulders, to find a creek crossing since snow piled high on either side and left a gash hip-deep where water still flowed, so you'd remove your skis, kick steps down, walk through water, then clamber back up.

Normally that'd be the way, but not this time. This time was so easy! We broke trail and hardly broke a sweat. We crossed creeks on sturdy limbs and glided through glades. I'd carried a Ziploc baggie of tools and miscellaneous repair items: steel wool and zip ties, wood screws and stubby screwdrivers, matchsticks to fill a stripped-out hole, string for everything—none of which we needed—and three mini bottles of tequila, which we shared at a junction less than a mile from the cabin, where they'd have to shovel their way down to the door. They had a long day of work yet ahead. I only had to ski six miles home.

I turned back one last time to see their faces blurred by flakes, their colorful hats and coats, and to wave one ski pole high in farewell as I left to care for the cat. I'd worn plastic boots because my leather ones had begun to fall apart, and the plastic boots gave me control I'd never felt on the trail before. For the first time, I also wore earbuds.

The music churned, guitars grinding low, reverb like a snowstorm blur, "shoe-gaze" they call it, or "slow-core." The voice strained nasal and pleading, on the verge of falsetto. The snow fell steadily in wafer-like flakes, not too large, not too wet, and slow as cottonwood fluff in June. When I reached a steep winding section where I'd snowplowed always, every single time, I made a series of tight telemark turns and coasted through the forest to the unplowed road. The earbuds didn't loosen or tug, the bindings didn't slip, the overbusy brain did not dwell on danger or triumph or the quality of the light. Music seeped like breath, like sweat-steam through my shirt for miles. I stopped for a drink of water beside the tree in the river. Laurie appeared, and we talked about the magic snow and the sick cat, briefly. She slid out of sight, and I was alone.

Sometimes I wonder why we love the tree in the river so much. Is it nostalgia? Do we love it because it's a remnant of the way things used to be? Probably not. If pressed, few of us could remember what exactly it looked like, way back when. There are a lot of trees in this valley. I have my favorites, but this one was not one of them. Until now.

Maybe it's because of its hardiness. Like a boxer, leaning hard against the ropes, who will not go down, no matter what. Or maybe it's the unlikeliness that it's still there or that we are, any of us, after twenty years, twenty-five, and counting, despite the weather, the tourists, jobs held and lost, friends come and gone; despite wars, shootings, a black president, a Seahawks Super Bowl, and a sickeningly snowless winter. Who knew you'd outlive Michael Jackson and Prince, own one pair of pantyhose, three dozen pair of boots, eight pair of skis, and still ride the same bike? Still ride a bike! Maybe you look at the tree and it's something like a mirror: crooked and bedraggled but still on its feet.

Or maybe, by now, it's familiarity. The tree is something to look forward to, something to believe in, something that's there. We sometimes try to impress others, people from outside the valley. When they join us to slog on skis upvalley, we ramp up the excitement, build tension in the approach—you won't believe this!—then, standing atop the culvert, we try to get them to whistle through their teeth— would you look at that?—instead they look at us pityingly, So this is what passes as entertainment up here? They're right of course. They're also missing the point.

The tree stands! Who could've known? How is it even possible?

At home after the long ski, I settled in to read John McCain's autobiography—why this book, I can't say, but I'd long admired him, begrudgingly, this steadfast scowling survivor—and the cat, never a snuggler, crawled onto my lap, and together we sat on the corner of the couch closest to the windows as dusk fell before five, then later, as moonlight glowed through clouds. There'd come a day when I'd rethink my admiration for McCain, a day I'd regret leaving the crew alone instead of the cat, but regret is shifty, while memory fixes hard. I remember how tired I was from the long ski up, buzzed from the ski down, settled and hopeful.

I could picture the scene in the cabin: skiers slouching, legs outstretched, wet ski boots crossed, heads tipped toward the yellow kerosene glow, elbows table-propped, splintery chairs creaky and ever on the edge of shatter, sipping whiskey we'd stashed in a plastic bear-proof canister, under tampons and sardines, for these trips like pilgrimages, year after year, trips like battles, like badges, like smudged entries in the green government journal, wide-lined.

I could picture the scene the next morning nearly as clearly. The shovels hung high on a cleat on a fir beside the bridge, large D-handled snow shovels we'd replaced in summer more than once using climbing spurs and a lanyard. You'd remove a glove and reach high to loosen the rope and lower the shovels, careful not to let them slide into the creek. Finally, you'd step out onto the span, trudge boot-top deep slowly, gingerly, to line out on the loaf-top mound. You'd turn the shovel upside down to chop a fault line from which chunks could fall and splash loudly into water, blue and translucent, arctic blue, icy blue, and rushing fast. Until, all at once, the overhang severs and drops, falling long in the winter sun, and crashes, leaving the bridge quivering, and everyone stone still.

So close. So close. They had not, luckily, been standing on the lip.

Over and over, I replay the day. The snow fell in a blur and the guitar played reverb slow and low and my skis moved easily in the up tracks and out over the creeks, across the bridges, to the falsetto straining, teasing, yearning, the drums thrumming, the soundtrack to transition. The next few years would be drenched in grief. Friends died, often unexpected, of cancer, heart attack, plane crash, pneumonia, suicide. And in the wider world, wars escalated, police shot kids, terrorists attacked nightclubs, fires and floods and mudslides wreaked havoc. But my friends are still here. Laurie is still here. North Fork Bridge stands. Even McCain, bless his ornery heart, same as he ever was. Only the cat, Daisy, is gone, replaced by happenstance by one nearly identical.

We know someday the tree will topple. We've even considered taking bets on when. But if we'd started taking bets back when we started talking about it, by now everyone would've lost.

People like to predict when trees will fall. The year after a big wildfire, they'd tell us: Better bring a lot of saw gas. But the roots of the blackened trees took years to loosen and sometimes never loosened at all. Snags line trails for miles on steep, burned-over side slopes, in wind-prone ridges, they stand straight and stubborn. Elsewhere seemingly healthy trees snapped by the dozen. Trees fell for unexpected reasons—a pestilence in the willows, a freak snowstorm in the spring—or for no reason at all. We gave up trying to guess.

But it's a hard habit to break, speculation. We must be hardwired for it. Lately there's been a glut of apocalyptic books and movies. *Station Eleven* and *MaddAddam, Mad Max* and the *Hunger Games*. Things are bad, and we will either triumph or suffer. The end is caused by a pandemic flu or a war or a natural disaster. The fascination lies in predicting who will survive and how and for how long. Some people bet on food production, some on weaponry, some on self-reliance, some on cooperation. A few outliers put faith in art.

I wrote one myself, a handbook of sorts that began as a list of skills for the post-oil world and morphed into a list of whimsical skills ostensibly for the end of the world: sleeping, reading, revising, storytelling. Reviewers spared no fury. These were not survival skills! Take this seriously! The book avoided guns, drones, and computers. Real preppers seem to believe in one or the other, weaponry or cleverness. I put stock in neither, only humanity. Do no harm. Make something. Laugh. We don't know what will happen or when. Even while we try to hold it together, to prep and plan, we don't know.

Meanwhile, remnants surround us. The meadow that didn't burn, the sandy ocean bluff sloughing but not yet slid, the eerie glowing coals in a campfire in the rain, the blackened toenail after a too-long hike, right before it peels off. Something to cherish, something that can't last. You come around one last bend before the view opens wide. You look up and catch your breath. There it is, still standing, silhouetted white against the cloudless blue.

The Injured Bear

AN INJURED BEAR LIVED IN THE ORCHARD. THIS SHOULD be no surprise. Bears have frequented the orchard every apple season for decades despite a rash of bear-proofing measures from electric fences to removing all the apples to hazing with firecrackers. So bears aren't a surprise, and they don't usually stop locals in their tracks. But this bear did.

He was a big black bear—250 pounds, maybe 300—or he had been earlier in the season before he got hurt. Now as autumn neared, he hop-walked from tree to tree with his right rear paw held high against his belly, and he grew skinnier by the day, which made him look lanky and disconcertingly human. The urge to weep or to toss him a dozen apples or—the most realistic option—to shoot him and get it over with was almost unbearable.

But why?

My mother taught me, in no uncertain terms, that animals aren't people. She did not abide anthropomorphizing, in part because of Catholicism—the "animals have no souls" bit from before Pope Francis suggested pets could go to heaven—and mostly because of her deep commitment to social justice. She's worked her entire life, in various ways, to make life better for those who are hungry, homeless, imprisoned, persecuted. For humans. We had no "save the whales" stickers in our house, no Audubon calendar. We watched *Mutual of Omaha's Wild Kingdom*, of course, but with the same detachment as when we watched *The Wonderful World of Disney*. The rhinos and hyenas were separated from us by continents and, more importantly, by cognitive ability. The point was plain even if no one harped on it. People think, pray, love. Animals don't.

Mom would not have abided house pets except for our infernal pestering, my siblings and mine. We pleaded until our parents could take it no more. The dog we picked up from the animal shelter on my tenth birthday answered to two names: Junior, which I called her with typical little-kid gender confusion, and Damned Dog, which my mother called her. Junior was poorly treated—never allowed indoors and walked sporadically.

I have friends who pamper their pets immoderately and others who admonish them behind their backs. Dogs

are dogs, they say. Sheesh. Don't let them sleep on pillows!
Don't feed them skinless boneless breast meat! Come on!
Americans spend $60 billion a year to spoil our pets, and
I'm not immune. We inherited our latest cat, Joon—a male,
more gender confusion—when a neighbor died, though
we'd sworn never to own a cat again, and we tried at first
to keep him on dried food, but once we found out he liked
canned food better, we caved. He's family in our childless
home. He sleeps on the pillows, even though I'm allergic. A
pile of used Kleenex surrounds the bed, and each morning
I awake with my eyes red and puffy, nursing a nasty hang-
over from Benadryl sleep.

Still, until recently, I never considered myself an animal
lover. An animal admirer, sure. Because of where I've lived,
and where I've traveled, and plain privilege besides, I've
seen a lot of animals in the wild: bear, elk, moose, wolves,
cougar, eagles, osprey, herons, deer, coyotes, bobcats, raccoon, possum, mink and marten, otters and beaver, gray
whales and orcas, sea turtles and alligators, pileated woodpeckers, Clark's nutcrackers, American dippers. The list
could go on and on, but even quantifying feels wrong, not
just bragging but tagging or bagging, like owning or con-
quering or maybe just knowing something unknowable.
I've always found human reactions to wild animals disconcerting. People fetishize them and idolize them with sea
turtle trinkets and howling wolf T-shirts, and sometimes
they wish to commune with them. (Though in my experience wild animals, like house cats and celebrities, usually

avoid those most eager for communion.) The topic, in general, seemed fraught. Maybe that's why I shied from writing about them. For many years I wrote nature essays, about trees, mountains, rivers, lakes, deserts, plants, even fire but rarely about animals.

Then, the summer the injured bear arrived, I had a series of encounters. One day a rattlesnake struck my bicycle spokes. Not long after, a mountain goat charged my car. I watched a gray whale breach and an elephant seal scratch its whiskery chin, both up close. A coyote gave birth in a crevice between boulders near my house, and tiny pups trotted past me as I worked rock-facing the foundation, hands amuck with mortar. I couldn't run for a camera. I just knelt forward and watched in wonder as they sniffed one log to the next and wrestled one another and turned to go when they heard their mother howl like our moms calling us in when the streetlights came on. And one day when nothing was going right, nothing at all, a red fox curled in a lawn chair and looked me right in the eye. Suddenly everything changed. Phone calls were answered, plans fell into place. I had no explanation. None. But I was grateful.

Then came this bear. Gimpy, we called him, to try to make the situation sound casual. But it wasn't. I'd stop to watch him in the morning while I was out running. I couldn't help myself. He'd hop a few steps, lie in the tall grass, and then he'd hop some more. Even when most of the apples disappeared, and all other bears left to gorge on spawning Kokanee, Gimpy stayed. He couldn't even make the quarter-mile trek to the river, and he surely couldn't catch a wriggling fish. A visitor went to the ranger station to report that the bear had approached him, that it seemed to be beseeching him, asking for help, and everyone was skeptical. The injured bear would not approach a human; he'd been firecracker-hazed too often. If he did approach a human, it would probably be because a bear's eyesight is famously poor. The beseeching seemed unlikely. But the feeling of being beseeched, well, we'd all felt it.

Years ago, when Damned Dog was dying, my mother finally let her inside. The dog went straight to my bed and curled up, Mom said, though she'd never been in the house and shouldn't have known which room had been mine, and anyway, I'd left for college months before. But we were connected somehow, Junior and I. Some lonely afternoons after school I walked her on a long chain to the empty field between our house and the Catholic church and let her off to run, and I ran after her. I taught her to high-jump in the backyard. She was treated as an animal, yes, but she was loved too. If my mother wouldn't use that word, she felt something. She was, after all, the one who actually fed the dog—I was too young, too irresponsible, and feeding the dog was easier for Mom than nagging me—and in the end she felt that she owed this fellow creature something, her sympathy at least, maybe her mercy.

That's how we felt watching Gimpy. We'd heard rumors that the Fish and Game guys were on their way because they feared Gimpy might pose a danger if he were to feel threatened. That, too, seemed unlikely, but if it gave the men an excuse to do what must be done, then so be it. We wanted it to be over.

Gimpy, of course, was not the only animal we'd seen suffer. There'd been a young buck abandoned by his mother, raised as part and not part of the herd, his haunches stained with diarrhea, never growing quite big enough, until one day he disappeared and died naturally out of sight, unlike the deer who ran into the orchard fence, tangling herself, and died thrashing in the hot sun right in front of our eyes. One year on Laurie's birthday we hit a mallard with our pickup, maiming it horribly, and Laurie had to beat it to death with the sole of her boot. Once a large buck got his antlers tangled in the parachute cord we'd used to hang our food from bears and, after a short struggle, strangled himself. You'd think over time you'd learn hardness, but in my experience, it often goes the other way. We know several men who used to hunt who can't anymore, some who can't even butcher chickens. They're done with it.

Lately a strange thing has begun to happen. I see a wild creature and I think of Joon, as though my love for him opens a spigot of compassion. The mere sight of a loon diving or an osprey soaring or a fawn stotting across kinnikinnick can make me weep. They move with the same muscular grace as the cat; their reflexes are somehow familiar to me; the way my nieces in a swimming pool remind me so much of my brother or sister as kids that a lump lodges hard in my throat. I know these comparisons are heresy to some: wild and domestic, human and animal. I'm not defending them intellectually, only acknowledging how it feels. My heart skips and dives. I feel the warmth of Joon's fur, how his tail whips while chasing a string or how his haunches grow taut when he climbs a tree for no reason, apparently, other than glee, and so by extension—who knows why?—I feel a kinship with the newborn fawns curled in the ditches in the orchard, with the swallows that flit and dive at the lake surface while I swim, and the bottom-feeders that lurk beneath me. I thrill at tiny rodent tracks in the snow, and grieve the carcasses Joon brings in as gifts. See? I've become one of them, the animal lovers: tender, irrational, stubborn.

I've heard that those who have intense affection for animals were once mistreated or bullied, so they nurture a reflex for the defenseless, the need to fight for the weak. But I've never been mistreated in any serious way. Then there's the argument about unconditional love and how animals have no bad in them, no malice. I don't know how we gauge this. Wild animals, in particular, may not be vicious, but they can hurt us. I don't have any way to know, for example, how malicious Gimpy was, but he was almost certainly more powerful than I am, since I'm a smallish woman who does not own a firearm.

Which brings up the horrid unspoken question: How did the injury happen? And the obvious answer. Someone shot the bear. Some people wanted to blame a hunter, which was certainly plausible. Bear season starts early here, at the beginning of August, and an irresponsible hunter could've hit the bear enough to hurt him and then been unable or unwilling or too damned lazy to finish the job.

We didn't know for sure, but the possibility bothered me more than I could admit. Laurie and I spent years defending hunters, empathizing with them, siding with them, defending them from soft-hearted city liberals. We had a bow-hunting neighbor, perhaps the kindest, gentlest man I've ever known, who lived for the week each year when he could spend his vacation hunkered in a snowy blind, shivering, to watch elk on the move, hoping to kill one. More often than not, he came home empty-handed. We knew others who literally fed their children on a once-a-year buck or bull or bear rather than feed them factory farm pseudo-meat—hot dogs or bologna or hormone-filled hens. We cheered them for their ethics, but we went overboard too. Especially when it came to bears. For a long time, too long, we thought it was fine to see bears shot, not only because they'd provide sustenance to children, but because they were annoying—they broke down trees and branches in the orchard, dug in compost bins, broke down garden fences—and mostly because they seemed, on some level, disposable.

That was before Rome Beauty. We weren't in the habit of naming bears—a poor practice, ever, with wild animals—but a local wildlife biologist did and the name stuck. Rome Beauty was fat, immune to humans, with amber highlights in her brown coat, and she hung around the orchard for

years, a decade maybe—hence her apple variety name—
and she gave birth every year, often to three cubs, the
indication of a well-fed sow. After a while, we expected to
see her, like a larger-than-life aunt, a diva, a presence not
to be ignored. Even regular summer visitors, family and
friends, knew the bear and looked forward to a sighting.
One year a hunter arrived on the ferry, rushed to the kinnikinnick patch right by the road, in plain sight, between
the waterfall and the orchard where Rome Beauty roamed,
shot her dead, then tried to remove her coat—now a trophy,
a rug-to-be—and race back to catch the ferry, leaving the
cubs orphaned and the carcass to rot. The man had, offi-
cially, done nothing wrong. While killing a sow and leaving
cubs is poor ethics, it's not illegal. Rumors circulated that
the hunter had to charter a private boat to avoid the disdain he'd face at the boat landing from hunters and non-
hunters alike; a ranger tried to help him pack at least some
meat on ice in a cooler. But none of that mattered. The deed
was done. The cubs hung on, starving, into the fall, when
biologists trapped them and sent them to a sanctuary, to
provide a bittersweet coda to the heinous story. Or at least
some solace.

How could I have believed our bears would last forever? Did I really believe there were enough to spare, so
many that we could accommodate hunters who'd show up
for an hour and leave with a rug? How hardened had we
become? Now there are fewer, and I miss them. I've come
to side with the creatures, even the Canada geese who line

the road squawking in spring as I jog past, protecting their nests in the cutbank below, even though some friends from the city despise them for their poop in the park. The geese are annoying, disposable, they must presume, and on some level extraneous. I'm not yet a Buddhist, but I don't want to make that mistake again. I'd rather error on the side of compassion.

Sometimes I have wanted to argue with my mother, to say compassion is compassion is compassion. I've wanted to say that I think people who love animals may have more to give to children or others, that learning to feel sorry for Gimpy might, say, help us feel for Syrian refugees. I'm not sure that's true for everyone. Consider the sheer uncontained rage people spewed at the Minnesota dentist who famously killed Cecil the lion. Cecil was a large charismatic mammal, singular and regal, maybe even godlike in the vein of Aslan or Simba. Plus there was only one of him, so there was no chance for a "collapse of compassion," the inability to deal with suffering on a grand scale, like in Rwanda or Darfur. There's rarely that kind of outcry, as Black Lives Matter activists rightly point out, seething with exasperation, when one human is lost. I can't speak for the whole of humanity. I can only speak for myself. Compassion seems to compound. The more I have, the more I have.

While our last cat, Daisy, was dying, I was away. I was sitting by my mother's side in California nursing her through a hard bout with cancer, while Laurie took sick leave to stay home with the cat. Meanwhile out in the late winter snow, a homeless man who had been stealing peanut butter from cabins was on the lam. A posse of locals chased him post-holing through the snow with guns. They passed Laurie's window, improbably, like goofy characters in a comedy Western. They only made her sadder. When the posse caught the man, rumor held they sent him to church and asked him to pray for forgiveness. I am not sure that approach counts as mercy, but it's probably better than turning him over to the sheriff. There's a way we wield compassion like power that makes me cringe too.

Daisy didn't last. Laurie couldn't bear to put her in a kennel and subject her to the torture of a boat ride to go to the vet downlake, nor could she shoot her. So Laurie waited, while the cat lost use of her legs and dragged herself crying, through urine, across the floor, and beyond. For days. I can't write it without weeping. Who could? When I returned home I sobbed for days, longer and harder than I'd cried for my sick mother or for all the friends who'd died in recent years, maybe in my life, and maybe I was crying for them, for all suffering and all loss, by proxy or permission.

Gimpy's body was discovered along a trail across the river from the orchard. The hole in his gut, an unmistakable bullet wound. How he'd managed to cross the river, hard to say. Neighbors suspected, in the end, that he had not been injured by a hunter but by a homeowner protecting chickens or a garden, firing from a porch, meaning only to maim. It's been years now, but I think of him often, and when I do, I feel sick and sad, cautioned and complicit, and grateful, too, that in the end, there was not just one bullet hole but two. A hunter came upon him and did the deed quietly. Put the poor bear, as the saying goes, out of his misery.

Flight Delay

HERE'S HOW IT BEGINS: IN THE WINDOW SEAT, LOOKING down, you're eight years old, maybe twelve, no longer small, not quite big, somewhere on the long cusp of change. The plane bounces hard and banks around Mount Baldy and descends for Ontario, California, a small airport—just a couple of gates, so small you take stairs down to the tarmac—as the vast sprawl unfolds. Eight-lane freeways crossing a dry riverbed, shopping malls, race tracks, truck warehouses and subdivisions and ball fields, the ocean unseen on the horizon, the desert at your back, tailwinds whipping, Santa Anas off the Mojave. The plane tips one way then the next, skips and teeters toward the ground.

Never again, you think. Please, you pray, get me out of here.

For years after that, you fly only rarely with a plastic water bottle full of gin, a Walkman to play loud, and a rosary to clutch. You dread the moment the pilot buzzes for his meal (shouldn't he be flying not eating?) and when he (always he) announces the cruising elevation (thirty thousand feet is too far to fall) and especially after 9/11, those ten, miserable music-less minutes at takeoff and landing when all devices must be shut off. You cry often and grasp the hands of strangers.

Once on a short jaunt from Southern California to Phoenix, the plane rises then, too soon, descends fast. The little boy in the window seat announces exuberantly: "Down, down, down, we're going down!" His mother shushes him, eyes the water bottle and rosary, and whispers to him.

"Look, lady," he cries. He turns and kisses the side of the plane. "We're not gonna crash. We're gonna be fine."

You think, How the hell does he know?

You can plan a trip and tell yourself you won't be afraid. You can wander through an airport with no anxiety whatsoever, shopping for the current issue of *Rolling Stone,* a treat reserved strictly for plane rides. Even as you take your seat. Fine. Even as you taxi faster and faster and faster. All good. Then you begin to rise, and fear rises like bile. You recite Hail Marys rapid-fire not to stave off death but to prepare for it.

But you can't go on like that forever. There are ailing relatives to nurse, godchildren to be baptized, book readings in Utah, conferences in Ohio, beaches in Mexico, and to attend to these pressing matters there are little white pills, cut in half, prescribed by a doctor. Shoes off, coat in the bin, baggie of liquids, laptop exposed. No knives. Never a knife. Moving fast, racing to the gate, stopping for Spam musubi on concourse C on the way to concourse D before they run out because they always run out.

When you know where to find the Spam musubi at SeaTac, you fly too much.

One summer morning not long ago, my flight out of Wenatchee, an airport even smaller than Ontario—single gate, no bar, and four flights a day—was delayed. I'd been delayed before, of course. Once, after four long stuffy runway hours in Houston, the pilot took off and dodged thunderheads as though steering a spacecraft through asteroids in a video game. Once, after two hours on the ground in Madrid, the pilot announced the plane was missing a part, and we'd be required to cross the Atlantic entirely below ten thousand feet, as often as possible above land. We flew over Iceland, which was green, and Greenland, which was icy, and landed fourteen hours later at Kennedy to change crews before continuing to Atlanta. You get my drift. Flight delays, in my experience, did not bode well.

But this time I was not alone. My best friend from childhood was traveling with me, and by happenstance we ran into an old friend from Stehekin—one who'd moved on but returned on occasion to visit—and we were not on a distant continent, not even in sticky-hot Houston, but in close, familiar dry-hot Wenatchee. Best of all, we could sit outside at a picnic table under a metal shade awning.

Officials explained that our plane needed a part that would be flown in from Seattle on the second flight of the day. The flight arrived with no part. We were awaiting the third flight—the fifth hour of waiting—when my old friend decided to jog to the nearest mini-mart for beer, bless her, a good couple miles away. This sort of spontaneity, I remembered, was what I'd loved best about her, even when it bordered on foolhardy. We were very hot. We were very bored. Beer would help. A dozen of us, the other passengers now our tribe, handed her fistfuls of sweaty cash, and she set off in her city shoes at a slow steady lope. We sat with nothing to do, read novels, paced circles, watched cloud shadows skate over green irrigated orchards atop brown hills. Time slowed.

For many years, I aspired to slowness, a kind of Thoreau-esque close knowledge of one small place. I walked to work every day—uphill in the morning, downhill in the evening—on one of two hundred or so miles of trails my crew maintained, every single inch of them familiar. The rock under which a rattlesnake lived, the switchback where a patch of white-barked aspens sprouted from talus, the place where the packhorses ate my lunch, the place where a gas can caught fire. Often we hiked for long hours, or for days, to where the forest opened up to postcard views, and since there's precious little work for a trail crew to do above tree line, we immediately turned around. I swore that when I quit I'd hike regularly for fun and never stop until I reached the high passes and ridgetops. But I don't. There's drudgery in measuring every close-known inch, and there's something more. People like to romanticize walking—Thoreau again—and while it's true that I had a lot of room to think, tons of it, miles and miles and miles, I had too little to stimulate my too-familiar thoughts—What's in my pack? What's for dinner? What work got done? What work is left to do?—on a never-ending loop occasionally broken by ancient AM radio song lyrics. One thing no one tells you about close knowledge is that it can be boring as hell.

Another flight. The plastic interior shudders at takeoff and Mount Rainier materializes immense above the clouds. The girl in ripped jeans beside me pulls out her iPad to capture it and holds the screen aloft for many long minutes. I am listening to music and trying to awaken that place in me that aspires. Aspires to capture beauty, to believe in humanity, to grow and change and muse and love and create. Before the day ends, we'll roar past the Rockies and the Chicago skyline shimmering and a stunning sunset over Lake Erie.

I am lonelier in the air than anywhere, and I often cry, still. For the beauty. For the disconnect. The land is there, right there, and so distant. You're crowded elbow-jab close with people you don't know, people you'll never know, overhearing their plans—the woman behind me will see a Barry Manilow concert with her mother, and she can hardly wait—as the Earth unfurls beneath you, the same Earth you're threatening by burning all this frivolous jet fuel. I used to be unable to look. Now, with the help of the tiny half pill, I enjoy looking. I can't help looking. If I don't get a window seat, I embarrass myself leaning over strangers to gawk. If, god forbid, they close the shade, I am lost.

The shapeliness of the land tears at me. The starkness of the Idaho mountains pocked with placid lakes. The brown squares of Dakota farmland rutted with rivers, vein-like more prominent than highways. The green carpet of the Piedmonts cresting toward cities crowding the coast. The land is big, bigger than the girl can fit in the frame of her iPad, bigger than I can fathom. I'm happy to be reminded of this, to marvel in wonder, because most of the time, with most people I know, bigness is bad.

Some hate big corporations. Walmart putting Main Street out of business and Amazon closing down indie bookstores and demanding cut rates from publishers, and the banks, most of all, raking in profits with zeros lined up like measures of distance between galaxies, for doing no apparent work whatsoever. Others hate big government with the feds bullying private business owners, spying on citizens, squandering taxes on lethargy. In defense, anyone can justify why big business and big government behave as they do. To spur innovation and efficiency! To preserve civil rights and wild lands! But both aspire to expand, or people aspire to expand them, and in the way of expansion, always, there are other people.

That's the problem with aspiration, I tell myself. It leads to bigness.

I was never afraid of crashing. I could fly in a helicopter—and sometimes did as a trail worker or seasonal firefighter—without breaking a sweat. That makes no sense, people told me. Flying in a jet is way safer than flying in a helicopter. I know. I know. But from the front seat of a helicopter, in a flight suit and helmet, you can see treetops through glass below your feet, clear enough to name the species—fir, pine, hemlock, spruce—and you can watch every move the pilot makes. You can adjust the air vent, you can talk over the intercom. See? You can feign some semblance of control. I did not like jets—do not like them still, half pill be damned—because I lack control, and I have no control over my lack of control over not being in control. Everything, absolutely everything, is bigger than me.

Sometimes I land in Ontario since my mom still lives in nearby Riverside. The plane skims the back side of Mount Baldy and nods to the Mojave as it banks for westerly descent. I brace myself for the wind. This much I know: the bad flight in my bone-deep memory occurred around the same time my dad dropped dead, suddenly and unexpectedly, while out running. It doesn't take a shrink to imagine how something like that—talk about loss of control—might meld with one wind-driven landing and manifest as phobia. In the final approach, we roar in over the Santa Ana

River, the river for which my hometown is named, the one I often describe as dry. But it's not dry at all. It's a reservoir, the underground water supply for the city. From the air you cannot see much water, only a trickle; bamboo obscures the channel and hides wild pigs and houses the homeless. Nothing is exactly in the open. You have to look hard to see what's there. Sometimes I think this is what's happened, after thirty years I've begun to get over the loss, to reach out from slowness and smallness as safety, to take another look.

There it is, the redemptive arc, triumph, rising above!

But another voice intrudes. Was the fear so unreasonable? Humans went millennia without flying. If, as some scientists now posit, memory is passed on for generations, fear of flying makes perfectly good sense. How many of our ancestors fell to their deaths off cliffs or into crevasses? How many watched with envy as birds of prey soared, how many watched with pure earthbound terror? Anyway, I'm not the only one who's scared. Planes often grow eerily silent during takeoff and turbulence, as everyone ponders, for a moment, the possibility that this will be it, all there is.

Then there's the moral argument. Flying causes 4 to 9 percent of climate gases and, because it sends emissions higher in the atmosphere than vehicles or coal plants, the effect might be worse yet. Sometimes I chide myself: Give it up. Give it up. But in the end, it would be only me—me and, say, the flip-flopped families on their way to Disneyland—who would give it up, leaving the airways to the wing-tipped executives or the tight-jeans-and-tennies tech guys who waltz to the front of the line—Group A, First Class, MVP members. Are they giving it up? They are not. Here is my sad secret fear: I'm not going to change a damned thing by not flying in an airplane. The government could change things in a heartbeat. Ditto the big oil companies. But me? To believe I could may be as foolish as thinking a helicopter is safer than a 747. But can't we admit this much? There's plain wrongness in your feet being lifted so far off the ground.

The pope kisses the ground when he lands, palms flat, clean white robes beside oil-glazed rain puddles or jagged potholes. Shiny dress shoes surround him in photos as he bows to the earth. Sometimes I fantasize about doing the same, slipping through the sunlit crack by the airplane door and hopping onto the tarmac, escaping the ridiculous tunnel, the long roller-bag walk into spaces devoid of fresh air, devoid of vegetation, devoid of culture, the sole indication of where you are appears on T-shirts in the gift shops or logos on ball caps. I used to think, after a turbulent flight, I might just walk away. More than once during layovers in Oakland or Dallas or Chicago, I considered finding my way to the Greyhound station. But I never did. I was too impatient. I had places I had to be.

Memories of waiting stick harder than most. Walking small-town streets while your car gets repaired, sitting outside the operating room or the delivery room, the last minutes of the last day of senior year, the long seconds before the starting gun goes off. You notice every last detail, the hazy sky scarred by contrails, the disinfectant or the diesel exhaust, the air-conditioning whirr, the gum-stuck quarter in the gutter. The arrival, at last, of your old friend, sooner than expected, with a twelve-pack tucked under one arm, having hitchhiked back up the hill with the local sheriff close on her trail. How to proceed? Surely, this would count as illegal public drinking, but no one was driving, and the day was hot, and the beer was cold. She tore open the box atop the picnic table and offered the sheriff a cold one, bless her, and he declined, but stayed close, leaning against a post under a metal awning, ignoring the beer, passing the time.

It's the kind of story I like to tell, one that illustrates how you have more freedom when you keep things small and more tolerance too. You can't judge so easily face-to-face. You're less likely to distrust. You don't have the constraints (bigger regulations) or demands (bigger profits) that lead to frustrations that lead to abuses. But that insight is as small as the story. Small in a good way. Small in a bad way. A helicopter is more maneuverable than a 747, but it can't go as far.

Sometimes you think this is how it ends. On the ground looking up. At home, planes leave wide contrail stripes across fir-fringed patches of blue. You can hear the noise but you can see neither the machines nor the passengers, sleeping or gawking, grieving or anticipating. If you hear the noise at night, you will you dream a too-familiar dream of an airport gone feral, an abandoned place, half-demolished, where jets take off and land too close over the heads of pedestrians. The noise deafens and tree limbs flutter and no one seems as worried as they ought to be. No one seems to notice the danger. When you realize in the dream that it is a dream, and so familiar, you think, Not this one again.

Please, you pray, get me out of here.

Instead, in an hour or so, your plane will arrive. A jet with props, two seats per side, twenty-two rows. Neither airliner nor helicopter. You'll climb the stairs from hard, hot ground and buckle your belt and rise fast with a chest-swoop gasp over silver-blue rivers and gray granite peaks that would take days to reach on foot. You'll lean your forehead against the window and shiver with awe at the bigness of what we don't yet understand, what we'll never know or achieve or control, and the sheer terror of looking down, watching the land recede.

Together We Pause

A CROWD GATHERED BY A WALL OF WINDOWS STARING out. Our plane had just arrived at the gate. Because it was early summer on a budget carrier, fewer business passengers waited than usual, more families, plenty of kids with movie-themed backpacks, and there'd be no empty seats on the plane. We'd take a short hop to Oakland and then transfer to Seattle, Denver, Minneapolis, and beyond. With the boarding call expected any minute, the waiting area should have been loud and lively, but I emerged from the bathroom to utter silence. No announcements over the intercom. No roller bags clattering or cell phone jangling.

Just this crowd, three rows deep, shielding their eyes with their hands.

I stood on tiptoes to try to see, but I could not.

"What's going on?" I whispered.

No one replied.

I'd seen a cop patrolling the terminal earlier, a local policeman fully uniformed, not TSA, so I wondered if there was a high-speed chase in progress on the tarmac—we weren't far from Los Angeles after all—or maybe a medical emergency. Part of me wanted to shy away, to allow who-ever faced trouble to face it alone, but curiosity got the best of me. I moved toward the windows and knelt to try to see through people's legs. As I did, I noticed that several men in the crowd had removed their ball caps and held them by their sides or over their hearts.

Then I could see. A flag-draped casket descended the baggage chute secured in a makeshift frame of two-by-fours, the most disconcerting sight imaginable on a week-day morning at a non-major airport. Soldiers marched forward, five men and one woman, in full dress uniform. They lifted the casket—the body—in unison and moved it to a rolling gurney. Then they stepped aside. Heat rose in waves from the asphalt. Nearby mountains stood barely visible, shrouded in wildfire smoke. All planes and vehi-cles and orange-vested employees stopped moving as two small station wagons approached.

The family emerged, a large family, young and old, apparently mixed race, arm in arm, well dressed. At the head of the queue, one woman, perhaps a mother, stum-bled in her heels whether from balance or heat or grief and took support from a large man, bald and impossibly muscular, who held her in a massive hunched-shoulder embrace, his necktie whipping in the wind furiously, while the rest of the family waited. When she rose again, they walked slowly together and approached the casket to have a moment to themselves.

With all of us.

We felt the guilt of voyeurism, the intrusion of privacy, but we couldn't turn away. This was, as they say, one of ours. How was it even possible? There'd been vague news from Mosul, yes, and skirmishes in Afghanistan. Less than a month since Memorial Day, and what did we remember, really, besides picnics?

Orlando. Mostly, we remembered Orlando. Two weeks earlier, a mass shooting had occurred in a nightclub. Even now, on soundless television screens hovering above us, CNN replayed a press conference with victims and their doctors. Between the clips of live footage, snapshots of those who died appeared, over and over, so youthful, some quite familiar after so many days of near continual coverage. Just before this trip, I'd managed to visit a memorial in a park in Seattle where messages in colored chalk covered the sidewalk and candles burned in the twilight. A group of young people, mixed gender, indeterminate gender, all leather and tattoos, smoked cigarettes and nodded kindly as we staid middle-aged people passed by reading the sidewalk-chalk tributes. My friend's husband held a vase of flowers his kids had given him as an early Father's Day gift, and he left them beside a candle that we could not per-suade to stay lit, and we bowed our heads, then left. Ever since the attack, communal grief, paired with stunned out-rage, had felt omnipresent on the radio, the television, the streets and somehow comforting.

But kneeling on stained utility carpet at the airport felt distinctly uncomfortable.

Fifteen years since 9/11. Fifteen years of war, and this admission feels both cliché and shameful: no one close to me had served. In Stehekin, where politics run red-hot but deeply insular, neither the libertarians nor the hippie lib-erals traveled downlake to the recruiting office spurred by outrage or patriotism or plain compassion for people a half globe away. Ditto for Riverside, where more mainstream politics and economic realities hold sway, no one I knew from there had served either. Even among my Midwest relatives, good patriotic Catholics, no one served.

But this soldier had. Not in the early aughts when the War on Terror dominated the news and soldiers died by the scores and politicians proclaimed their heroism, but right now, as the casualty numbers—for Americans at least—had thankfully dropped to single digits. As if every single digit was not, in fact, a precious human life. Who would remember?

We would. I looked at the kids, so many of them, held firmly at their parents' waists, staring out. They'd remem-ber, too.

Once before I experienced something similar in far different circumstances. I'd driven the long winding road amid green hills at Point Reyes National Seashore. Mine was the only car on the road for miles and near sunset reached a parking lot at the road end, which was inexplicably packed. I walked the last half mile to the dramatic lighthouse surrounded by sea on a wide paved trail, and I saw not one soul. I could not imagine where everyone hid. Suddenly, I came around the corner to where a very large crowd leaned against a chain-link fence in silence looking out.

"What's going on?" I whispered.

No one replied.

A man pointed toward the sea, and I gazed out for a silent minute until a gray whale surfaced, then another, then another, more gray whales than I'd ever seen in my life.

Gray whales migrate semiannually five to seven thousand miles one way, a long, slow commute, the longest commute of any mammal, but not the loneliest. They travel in pods from their summer feeding grounds in Alaska to congregate in small lagoons in Baja California to breed and calve. The predilection to stick together is a big part of why they nearly went extinct in the late nineteenth century and again in the twenties; they were such easy prey all hunkered in those nursery lagoons. Official protections allowed them to recover enough to be removed from threatened status under the Endangered Species Act in 1995. Now the population is estimated at about twenty-two thousand. Whether that's sustainable is up for debate. Whether they are awesome to behold is not.

Before that evening at Point Reyes, I'd seen a few. Once from a sightseeing boat as a kid in a Dramamine stupor, once from a Molokai balcony with Laurie and my mom, and once from a bluff overlooking the Strait of Juan de Fuca among friends who decided mutually we'd seen one, though no one could be sure. But never so many all at once, and never in such an awe-riveted group of strangers.

The crowd oohed and aahed fireworks-style each time the whales surfaced, but did not otherwise speak. When they submerged, we stood in silent admiration, near reverence, waiting for them to surface again. They swam a long distance from us; no way would they be visible but for our vantage point so high on this wedge of land jutting seaward. So we saw no dramatic breaches—nothing camera worthy—just bodies rising in unison or sequence. We gasped each time.

This lasted forty-five minutes. Only when the light softened toward dusk and the whales moved too far north, too distant to see even as specks, and we began to disperse did I realize many people in the group did not speak English.

Patriotism sneaks up on you. When athletes stand on the podium at the Olympics and the national anthem begins to play. When you've traveled abroad for months and return home to the sight of an American flag rising in the wind. When you think of the litany of unlikely triumphs—Seneca Falls, Selma, Stonewall—and begin to believe maybe just maybe the arc of history does bend toward justice. Even when you kneel stiffly staring at a casket on the tarmac feeling far less pride than sorrow, even as Peter, Paul, and Mary plays on a loop in your mind from childhood. When will it ever end? That, too, counts.

Though I haven't known soldiers, I have known veterans. They receive preference for government jobs, including Park Service jobs. To stereotype is unfair, I know, but there's an undeniable thread of similarity. They're physically strong, capable, polite, and proud. Friendly, yes, but with a solemnity underneath too, a seriousness. Most have been in their thirties or close. They come for a while and leave, and at least one met a sad ending. Not that he's alone. Twenty veterans per day commit suicide—twenty!—leaving family and friends to grieve and to wonder at how carefree they once were.

Like the rest of us. Most of the time. We don't fret over wars or extinction. Instead, we vote and sign petitions, read and Tweet, and then plan summer vacations to splash in the waves and play cards on the screened deck while mosquitoes buzz just out of earshot until these moments come unbidden by the seaside or at a city park memorial where candles will not stay lit or in the parking lot when a double rainbow appears over a shopping mall. No need for tickets or turnstiles or intercom announcements. No planning or paying. We just stop. Together. Like a shared reflex. We don't even have to think about it.

One of ours. Two easy parts. There's one, a single digit, a precious life. In snapshots on a pixelated screen, in a box on the runway, in a pod heading north with whatever offspring can make the long trip. Then there's ours. Not mine, not my responsibility alone, not mine alone to celebrate or mourn. We have to face it together. So much we have to face. War, famine, climate change, extinction, injustice. It's all too much. Until it's not. It's right there in front of you. And suddenly it's ours.

Back on the tarmac, family members bowed their heads, fingered the edge of the flag, and wrapped themselves around each other as their hair and clothes grew disheveled in the heat and wind. Then, at last, they climbed back into the station wagon. The soldiers marched to the gurney and wheeled it toward a hearse, the back doors open and waiting. They lifted the casket into the hearse, which drove away followed by the family cars.

Inside the terminal, no one dared move. Kids fidgeted and were shushed. I'd been kneeling longer than I like to, but I stayed kneeling. Not long afterward, bags began to drop from the chute. A woman in shorts and an airline polo broke in to announce we should line up to board. Conversations started slow, cell phones appeared.

We walked through the tunnel, suspended over the tarmac below—safe from the heat and the wind and the jet-fuel fumes—no longer silent but not loud either. Once we sat and buckled ourselves in, the pilot spoke over the intercom, voice wavering, to say what an honor it was to have brought a soldier home to a final resting place. Meanwhile the rest of us were on the move to Oakland, Seattle, Denver, Minneapolis, and beyond. We taxied fast and lifted into the air, higher and higher, above the cities, then the mountains, strangers bound together, the binds loosening as smoke settled thick in the canyons.

Here in the WUI

ONE SUNDAY MORNING LATE LAST SUMMER, AS WILDFIRES burned in every direction, we gathered at the swim dock. Thick smoke hovered. Ash fell like snow. A dozen or so neighbors, ages eight to sixty-plus, stood in wetsuits or in knee socks waiting for the start of our first-ever Stehekin triathlon. One runner wore a multicolored yarn wig. Several bikes sported ribbons and streamers. Some participants would complete the entire course: half-mile lake swim, eight-mile bike, two-mile run. Others had formed makeshift teams. An unofficial official in a yellow hard hat and orange vest announced the only rule. There would be no rules.

When I moved to this valley, you could count on one hand the number of wildfires that had grown larger than a thousand acres in the past hundred years. Since then we've watched more than a hundred thousand acres burn in a fifty-mile radius from home. Of course we take the threat seriously. We started a volunteer fire district. We hold work parties to create so-called defensible space. We've attended workshops on Firewise principles. We've cleared dead vegetation, moved firewood piles, screened soffits, and cleared under decks. We've pruned ladder fuels—low-hanging dead limbs that can carry flames upward—from conifers and raked duff away from outbuildings. We drafted a Community Wildfire Protection Plan to integrate our efforts with state and federal land managers.

But at some point life goes on. For a couple of seasons, a few of us had been traveling to compete in triathlons, so when a local teenager proposed we have an event here, we thought, why not?

The unofficial official blew a whistle, and we splashed into the water swimming, stroking hard toward a yellow kayak marking the turnaround in which two more unofficial officials waved a big red flag. Breathe right and watch trees torch on the ridgetop. Breathe left and pass a cabin. Watch for the big red flag somewhere out in the smoke that seemed to stretch from Oregon to Canada, east to Montana or beyond. We arose dripping from the water while dogs nipped at our heels. Then bikers headed off past views of fire-scarred forest—black, silver, bronze, and rust—with fire names that echo in our collective memory: Wolverine, Flick Creek, Rainbow Bridge, Tolo.

The Boulder Fire, in 1994, was the first to come close. We sat on tailgates to watch the fiery fringe snake down a steep drainage three miles away. Sparks spewed into the night air as trees torched and flames leapt crown to crown from valley bottom to ridgetop, and then trickled back down, over and over. By day, we packed for evacuation fretfully and debated fire management until finally a late-season rainstorm put our fears to rest. Nowadays, like so many things in middle age, our response to fire is less emotional—less frantic and less awed—and more nuanced and pragmatic, whittled down to the nitty-gritty: trying to keep things running—the fire pump, the generator, the sprinklers on the roof—and remaining vigilant.

Fire, which used to be an occasional unruly visitor, has carved out a permanent place here in the Wildland Urban Interface. (Defined as areas where houses meet wild vegetation in the mountains or in the woods or in the sagebrush hills, the WUI—pronounced "woo-eee"—sounds a lot more fun than it is.) Back in 1988, when the National Park Service allowed a handful of wildfires in Yellowstone to burn into a 1.2-million-acre conflagration, the battle lines around fire became hard drawn. Scientists explained that too much fire suppression had made the forest unnatural in places where, for example, fire-dependent ponderosa pine gave way to shade-tolerant Douglas fir. Let it burn, they said. Meanwhile, those who lived in nearby communities saw their homes and livelihoods threatened. Put it out, they cried. Thirty years later, here in the WUI, those debates seem distant, nearly quaint. The all-or-nothing rhetoric has given way to reality. We can let some fires burn, yes, but not in August, not so close to town.

Commentators argue that the WUI is dangerous and costly and that those who live here need to take more responsibility for what it costs to fight the fires. Some say houses in the WUI should no longer be insured or built. Yes, all of that makes sense, but meanwhile this is our home. For years those voices, reverberating in the echo chamber of op-eds and later on social media, cemented in me and my fellow WUI-ites a stubborn contrariness. Even as we planned for the worst, I believed, like most of my neighbors—the men, at least—that I'd stay through evacuation, any evacuation. We knew people personally who'd saved houses, their own and their neighbors', by spraying garden hoses in flip-flops while firefighters backed out or focused attention elsewhere. With that in mind, who would not plan to stay?

Not me. Not anymore. It's scarier than it used to be. We watch the NOAA weather forecast and see the temperature rising astronomically, impossibly—isn't this the Pacific Northwest?—and the humidity dropping. Fuel temperature and moisture are listed, too, right there on the website, but some days, often, I cannot bear to look at those columns. We're set to leave at a moment's notice with a generator running, the passports in a manila folder, and the cat in a box. We wait for the sound of distant thunder, dreaded but not unexpected. All it takes is one close strike.

Days before the triathlon, the Wolverine Fire burned over Domke Lake where a lone longtime inhabitant lived in sparse isolation renting rustic cabins and canoes to weekend fishermen. When the fire came, he had no time to hike out. He rowed out into the center of the lake as he had always planned to do in such an emergency. The air singed his lungs. The word "ember" no long applied to flaming logs spinning from the sky. He dropped from the boat and submerged in the water, according to lore, and came up as necessary to take sips of throat-scalding air. And so he survived the night.

From the swim dock, as we awaited the bikes for the final handoff, we could see the ridges around Domke blackened and bare. The fire had burned so hot the earth was scalded, sterilized. By spring, it would look like the Sahara. The runners hit the pavement: shirtless teenage boys wincing with side aches, small kids sprinting limbs akimbo, middle-aged joggers weary and grinning. Just one leg left to go.

The plan at first had been to run on a trail, but that would've left spectators in the lurch. So we decided to run the road. If we had run a trail, we'd have passed blackened trunks surrounded by fireweed blooming pink and red ripe thimbleberries, the first plants in succession, so different from the forests they used to be. I remember when no trails in this valley looked burned. Now few aren't. Stories from the WUI most often focus on houses destroyed, communities displaced or rebuilt, but the landscape, too, has changed dramatically, astonishingly, and it's still changing.

Some of those fires were, of course, set on purpose, "prescribed" as they say. Firefighters line the road in fall or spring with drip torches, steel canisters of a diesel-gas mix to pour into the duff to set a low-intensity burn in hope of restoring forest health in a valley grown too thick after a hundred years of suppression. This is the now-familiar story in the American West. This, too: Try as we might, we in the WUI can't manage fire alone. We depend on the government for prescribed fire as much as for major suppression. So the tension remains. Who is responsible?

Not long after we started seeing large fires, I traveled to other mountain towns on vacation and was shocked to see A-frame cabins with cedar shake roofs and conifer limbs resting on eaves and gas cans stored in woodsheds. Was it nonchalance? Ignorance? Neglect? No telling. I could see then, clearly, the answer to those red-hot questions. Should the work of prevention be done by homeowners or contractors or volunteer groups or federal, state, or local governments? Yes, yes, yes, yes, yes, and yes.

Meanwhile, in the echo chamber, new ideas circulate. Maybe communities in the WUI should be seen instead, simply, as fire-dependent ecosystems. Native people have known as much for centuries. The Bureau of Indian Affairs in the Pacific Region has moved beyond Firewise to advocate for a new understanding of fire they call 4 Rights. Right Time: recognize that fire has different effects depending on the season and the weather. Right Place: integrate the needs of healthy forests, grasslands, streams, plants, animals, and people. Right People: involve multiple generations, youth as well as elders. Right Choice: make a conscious decision about when and where fires should burn. I have to admit I like the concept. Once, when doing research for a book set in the Sierra Nevada, I heard a moving story of young Maidu firefighters starting a prescribed burn with pine boughs, rather than drip torches, after receiving a blessing from elders. This seemed a way to accept fire, to integrate it into culture, and on some level to dodge all the blamey talk. But no matter how much we embrace fire in theory, it's not so easy to live with in real life.

On Facebook in the days following the triathlon, we received scoldings from near and far. *How unhealthful! You should stay indoors when air quality is that bad!* True enough. I take an inhaled steroid each morning. We live regularly through what doctors now call "smoke waves," days or weeks of skies black with particulates, expected to get exponentially worse in the decades to come and cause more sickness. The danger is real, but so is the danger of gun violence, flooding, traffic, stress. No place is immune to danger. If we stayed indoors all fire season, we would never emerge. Besides the teenager who organized the event would be leaving soon for school, and really, which is unhealthier, anxiety alone or exercise together?

In the weeks to come, bracken ferns browned to a crisp and clusters of maple seeds dangled like kindling. Leaves turned orange, and sunlight through the windows glowed orange, the gray road dust hovered orange, eerie as gaslit streets in Dickens's England. I stayed inside reading and stumbled upon a description of another fire right here in 1889 during which a visitor tried to ride upvalley and burned the legs of his pony so badly that he had to wrap them in ointment and bandages to keep the yellow jackets off. As he returned to the lake, the leather on his boots shrunken from heat, he gazed out at the smoke "which appeared to cover the face of the whole country."

There's an odd comfort in history, a reminder that much of the West is, indeed, a fire-dependent ecosystem. But there's also danger in believing that nothing has changed, that suppression and climate change have not colluded to create bigger fires, hotter, and yes, more dangerous. Within days of the triathlon, we'd hear the horrific reports from Twisp twenty-five miles east: three firefighters killed in a fast-moving fire started by dry birch leaves resting on a power line.

Meanwhile, a teenager ran between two orange cones to claim victory in a race with no reward. Afterward we ate pizza squares and ginger cookies and drank water served in empty jelly jars so there'd be no paper waste and posed for photos. We listened to strange silence since, for the first time in weeks, poor visibility kept helicopters on the ground. The omnipresent radio chatter was gone, too, the knob twisted to a click. We headed home to turn on the sprinklers and listen and await the blessed arrival of fall.

Fire One, Fire Two

THE FIRST TIME WAS ALL MAGIC. WE LAY ON OUR BELLIES and sighted the rifles, pulled back on bowstrings and let arrows fly. We sang off-key and sprinted hot asphalt to the pool, frog-kicked on our backs and squinted into sky where cracked-dirt foothills cradled the blue, then boosted by one armpit, shimmied up the saddle, reins in hand, high astride a real live horse, high on top of the world. Our dorm shone yellow with sunlight on steel cots in orderly rows. Our counselor, Betsy, strummed a twelve-string guitar on a rainbow strap. We slept hard, woke to reveille, saluted the flag, and prayed Our Father. In the cafeteria, Brother Vince served pancakes with syrup, single-sized boxes of Frosted Flakes, red fruit punch ladled out of a vat, as much as we wanted. Our lips laced with crimson, our veins raced with dextrose.

So what if I didn't know how to fold hospital corners? Couldn't learn to save my life. Each morning I stood at attention by my footlocker, arms straight-finger stiff by my sides, for inspection and waited with trepidation, not quite dread, because nothing bad happened. Nothing ever did.

Camp was nestled in desert hills wide and sandpaper bare. Against that background, the grounds splayed out lush and green, more manor than ranch. The chapel, a former ranch house, had been constructed from locally quarried granite eighteen inches thick. On even the hottest days, the chapel remained dark and cool and otherworldly as the lily ponds in full view from the altar. White rectangular panels lining the tops of the walls displayed the Stations of the Cross in carved marble. I craned my neck to see and try to name them. Jesus falls. Veronica wipes the face of Jesus. Bodies in motion, sinewy and intertwined with each other and the ever-present cross. Like a protest or a parade. Or maybe like camp.

My family attended Mass at this chapel each Sunday, so maybe that's why it did not feel strange to land here for an entire week as a six-year-old, why the memory occupies a safe private space: the smell of eucalyptus and horse manure and gunpowder fresh shot.

On the last day of the week, with our bags packed and stored, the counselors gathered everyone in a room for farewell festivities, and at the very end they called one name from the microphone onstage, just one, and through the long lens of time, I watch a shy girl, a very happy child, half jog to the front of the room, to accept congratulations like everyone's little sister, like a mascot of sorts. Not proud, not embarrassed, but astonished. For years I kept the certificate signed by Betsy. Camper of the Week. I wore my camp T-shirt with green lettering in faux wooden sticks until holes wore through the fabric and my mom tore it into rags.

Three years later, everything had changed.

The songs to start with. I'd learned they weren't even ours—"John Jacob Jingleheimer Schmidt," "Father Abraham," every camp had them. "Down in Our Hearts," all the Jesus camps had that one. The rifles were BB guns, the horses old and slow, the small sunlit little kids' dorm no longer mine. Instead, the big dorm with dozens of cots and the stench of bodies and a long wall of glass crisscrossed by metal bracing, spooky and shadowed.

At the pool, my wiry limbs would not allow me to float long enough to pass advanced beginners and move to intermediates. No matter that I could swim the strokes and leap from the high dive. No matter that the other advanced beginners were barely doggy paddling. Over and over, I tried to float but sank. I tried to get the hospital corners right too. I folded and tucked and refolded and stood at the foot of the bed only to have the sheets torn back in array. Try again! My locker was not tidy enough, my shoes wrongly tied. The infractions compounded. The other kids watched or sniggered or left to shoot guns, while I stayed inside to try again, my hands like clubs, so clumsy at the task, as I fought back tears.

At dinner, Brother Vince offered extra spaghetti, but I turned him down. I wasn't hungry. I wanted to go home. I thought about the word "homesickness" and how even thinking about it felt like defeat, like weakness. At the end of the week, I headed home, safe and grateful and utterly baffled. I had no idea what had gone wrong. I never went to camp again.

For years, I've carried dual memories into new situations: book readings, new jobs, even dinner parties. Anticipation borders on dread. The last moments before approaching the podium or ringing the doorbell, hors d'oeuvres in hand, I find myself thinking, Will it be like the first time at camp or the second, everything right—magic even—or everything wrong?

Camp left its mark. For most of early adulthood I made my living maintaining hiking trails in the backcountry. With a tent, not a cot; a saw, not a bow. Late in my career, I flew south to Kings Canyon National Park to attend blasting school. The training involved classroom time, endless calculations, higher-level math than I'd done since high school, and practice in the field: drilling holes in rock, meting out explosives, tying off the detonation cord—with a girth hitch never a clove—then stringing out yellow wire to carry the current. On the handheld radio, you called the

warnings in succession. Fire one. Fire two. Fire in the hole.
I'd blasted plenty before then but never found it exhilarating. Why all of a sudden? Why does the week stay with me
now? All sun-heated pine and the head-hit smell that lin-
gers after the shot and silver cold cans of beer in the dank
bunkhouse after work and the way the guys accepted me
as a kind of older sister and mascot. I've forgotten people
who worked with me for months, but I remember blasting
school. I remember the T-shirt I wore, several years old,
work-worn, sun-faded red, and soft as sleep. Why the fond-
ness? Within months I'd quit trail crew. Maybe it was the
nearness to the end? Or to a new beginning? The edges of
things always catch the brightest light.

The funky writing program was all magic. Classes met in
former army barracks with the Olympic Mountains on the
horizon. Ferries and barges passed on the steel-gray sheen
at dawn. Deer grazed on soccer fields. The rooms were
shabby, the vibe chummy. I visited as a guest speaker and
a year later joined the faculty. Shortly thereafter we moved
from the barracks to a historic inn.

The inn sat tucked among madronas and firs, ocean
spray and salal. It was rickety, remote, vaguely *Shining*-
esque. Thick moss lined the asphalt road edge, and black-
berries crawled cedar fences. The podium in the dining
room backed up to a wall of framed mirrors. During
nightly readings, as aspiring poets and novelists and essayists stood to read their work, some for the very first time,

we could see ourselves in funhouse fragments and behind us through windows the dark expanse of Penn Cove.

By day Penn Cove was a lively place. On the dock, otters flopped and turned, toying with a mooring rope. Seals lounged on mussel beds. Writers gathered under twisted red-barked madronas to talk about point of view, about assonance and dissonance, about how or where or when a story should end. A great horned owl hooted at night and dominated breakfast conversations. Who heard the owl? There were kingfishers and osprey and driftwood large as park benches stacked and strewn and weathered gray like the sky, gray like the sea. There were orcas in Penn Cove too, supposedly, also called killer whales, though we never saw them.

During the readings, if someone walked to the upstairs bathroom, the floorboards creaked loudly enough to drown the reader's voice. The inn was built in 1906 of local madrona logs. How they found enough of them big enough or straight enough, we'd never know, but the floor joists were old. By midweek in the nine-day residency, each writer would succumb, if briefly, to despair. Not enough ambition, or too much. Too much wine, or not enough dessert. Too much thinking and never, ever enough sleep.

The subtle shift, the downward turn. The moment I dread most. For thirty years, I've told myself it's mysterious, the thread-thin difference, entirely out of my control, having only to do with chemistry or the alignment of the stars.

At times, I could not shake the sense that the responsibility was my own—a challenge to face, a sentence to write, a bull's-eye to hit. If you fall, get up. If you miss, reload. Until recently when I started thinking about the second time at camp obsessively and began to suspect that the hospital corners were not the problem, nor the swim lessons, nor the songs, nor the weary old ponies. The Beef Lady was the problem.

A summer camp ritual. We're startled awake after dark in the big dorm by rowdy counselors who gather us in the middle of the room where the moon casts crisscrossed shadows, and there is no place to sit. We drape blankets over our shoulders and stand barefoot on linoleum. Some girls crowd in, others hover on the fringe.

The storyteller holds a flashlight to his face. He's the kind of counselor we all have crushes on, like the boys on the cover of *Tiger Beat*: Leif Garrett, Robby Benson, Matt Dillon. But he's not as pretty as them and seemingly not as kind. He sneers beneath his smile. He cackles when a listener gasps as the story unfolds: a ghost woman comes down from the hills and steals beef from Brother Vince and leaves a drippy bloody trail behind her when she goes. That's it.

But it is scary as hell. I tell myself it's made up. I tell myself it's plain stupid. But it's no good. The too-cute counselor describes the beef-bloody trails with exuberance, expresses concern for Brother Vince with sincerity, and soon the gauzy image lodges in my brain—she wears a

long white nightgown that drags in the dirt—and through-
out the night I'm shaken. I lie awake and see her clearly
walking barefoot in the moonlight past the chain-link
fence around the pool and past the rifle range and off-trail
through the crevice-hid cacti. The only way to sleep is to
devise a plan: I will find the storyteller in the morning and
I will demand the truth.

So, I do. And he leans in earnestly.

"I'm afraid it's true," he says.

I plead with the other counselors to rat him out, but
they refuse. I become the worst kind of sniveler, needy and
foot stamping, as the counselors ramp up the stakes, taking obvious glee in my terror as do the other campers once
word seeps out.

I was a lost cause. I was sunk.

Some people claimed the historic inn, too, was haunted by
ghosts, an old woman perhaps or a child whose tiny coffin
sat upstairs near the bathroom. I didn't buy it for a second.
I wouldn't fall for that again. I rose predawn to kayak with
a colleague in boats he built himself. Together we watched
the sun rise pink over Mount Baker, the clouds a swath
behind the peak. Once during each summer residency, students and faculty alike leapt in the frigid water and afterward stood shivering wrapped in towels. I was taking on
more responsibility, being groomed to take charge soon.
Assistant director. Next stop: Director. Everything was fine,
just fine.

Each evening, the faculty gathered for happy hour upstairs at the inn, sitting on the floor or on small hard chairs surrounded by walls of books, and there was something atavistic, literary, and close about those minutes. Downstairs, waiting for dinner then readings, students loitered around a fireplace as printers rattled and the screen door slammed hard and the front desk phone rang.

One year jellyfish appeared. Saucer-sized with egg-yolk centers, they pocked the surface of the water and stuck to our kayak paddles with every stroke as another story began to circulate quietly: mishandled funds, bungled administration, everything botched and badly, due to self-preservation or too-bold ambition or parochialism or all of the above.

In no time we'd be sunk.

In August 1970 a pod of orcas was herded into the dead end of Penn Cove. Six juveniles were captured to use as performers in marine park shows. Five others drowned. Some of the hunters are haunted by the anguished cries, the piercing screams of mothers trying to reach their calves, and calves tangled in nets trying to reach their mothers. You can hear these men tell their chilling tale forty years later on YouTube, how they filled the cavities of the dead ones with rocks, and lashed anchors to their tails and sank them. You can also hear the apologist, the leader of the catch, saying, "What more could I do? I didn't mean to kill them." It is harder to have sympathy for him than for the eighty circling animals crying unmistakably, flapping their flukes hard on the water surface as their babies are scooped from the water and lifted in nets onto the ship deck.

Again perspective shifts. Suspicion hardens toward conclusion. It's not about newness or gumption or a lack of self-confidence that shows in your aura as you try to fold the sheets or arrange the explosives or read your poem as the floors creak overhead. Sometimes there's actually something wrong. The counselors were jerks. The orcas were slaughtered. The moments of triumph, Camper of the Week, are fleeting and precious and, on some level, false.

A horse packer, a woman my size and my age, attended blasting school with me. On the flight south, she chattered excitedly about seeing orange groves in blossom and about the possibility, too, of seeing new birds. One woodpecker in particular. Her boyfriend, a birder, had told her to keep an eye out. So while making the calculations, drilling the rock, packing the holes, setting the blast, she kept an eye out. When it was her turn to press the button, the rest of us sat by our radios. Fire one. Fire two. Silence. We waited far too long. When would she say, "Fire in the hole"? What could possibly have gone wrong? The story came later. The woodpecker had appeared on a tree right above the rock to be blasted at the very moment she planned to press the button, and despite the peer pressure, despite the fact that we were the only girls in class, she held fire. If that blast had been mine, I would've blown the bird to smithereens.

On the last morning, I walked downstairs and stood before the wall of mirrors, wrote dates for the upcoming semester on a whiteboard, wished the students safe travels, packed my things, and left. I had no idea what was to come. That we who'd returned to this place, year after year, would return no more. That I'd spend weeks as suddenly-director, captain of a sinking ship, smoothing over wrinkles, steering a steady course, trying to make land, any land. People would demand the truth, and I'd give an unsatisfying answer. Not this: *If there were ghosts, I didn't see them.* So much as this: *There were ghosts. I should've seen them.*

Why would you give kids rifles and teach them to shoot anyway? We never questioned, and nothing ever went wrong, but what could possibly be the point? We didn't think enough about what guns could do. Ditto for explosives. Not until after September 11 (not even after Oklahoma City six years earlier) did it become dramatically more difficult to get your hands on powder. And anyway, most people use it for something good, possibly even banal. *If you're going to do it, do it well*, we thought. Instead of this: *Beware of the damage you might do.*

With that in mind, I tell myself to let go of this whole business of the first time at camp versus the second, and the thread-thin difference: same experience, same place, soured. But I cannot. There's too much unseen. Whenever the eternal reckoning subsides—What went wrong? When? How? What should I have known, understood, watched out for, done differently?—memories float back up unbidden.

We wrote and swam and laughed and drank wine in plastic cups among dusty volumes of Thackeray. One night at a party, a guitar appeared and my colleagues sang the blues with sweet voices, so high and clear. Who knew they could sing like that? How had I never known? Elated and hopeful, I walked back to the historic inn along the cove in the dark listening to the sound of water lapping on the shore.

See, how the innocence comes rushing back at you, intoxicating and insidious? Until you remember how easily it can happen. One moment you lay, belly in the dirt, rifle butt on your shoulder, the target straight ahead, and one moment later, smack in the middle of the bull's-eye—who knew?—a paper-torn hole, small as a dime.

Pierce

PICTURE HIM WITH A NOTEBOOK, ASTRIDE A HORSE, THE morning light cloud-streaked and pink above the rolling terrain. It's August 1882, and Lt. Henry Hubbard Pierce is set to begin an expedition from Fort Colville, Washington, in search of an elusive railroad route across the not-yet state, over the mountains and to the sea. He's under orders of Brig. Gen. Nelson A. Miles, commander of the Department of the Columbia, who is, in turn, under the orders of Gen. William Tecumseh Sherman.

His guide is Joe LaFleur, "a half breed ... with shrewdness as a pathfinder and perfect familiarity with all the Indian dialects from Colville to the Sound" who shows "remarkable endurance and cheerful energy." His illustrator is one Alfred Downing. Most of the rest of the names are lost to history.

Not far from where they begin, at Kettle Falls, they halt for a moment "to watch the lusty salmon make their persistent and stupendous leaps" and pass several lodges of Colville Indians drying salmon. Soon they cross the Okanogan River, so clear, Pierce notes, that every pebble can be seen, and they discover a broad swath of valley that Pierce says would be good for growing wheat, oats, potatoes, rye, and corn. Would be good because, actually, it already is.

> In plain view upon the opposite bank are eight
> comfortable ranches belonging to the Columbia Lake
> Indians, who raise grain and vegetables in consider-
> able quantities—no less than 4,000 bushels of wheat,
> said to be the best in the Colville country, having been
> harvested by them last year.

That night they find an Indian ranch, forty acres or so, and since no one seems to be around, they take the liberty of herding their animals for the night inside an enclosure. This is not pure happenstance. Part of their mission, besides finding the elusive route, is to show federal presence, flaunt it maybe, and to gauge the resistance or acceptance of the Native Americans. No one balks at them using the pen. Chalk one up for acceptance.

I read the section and reread it, trying to gauge my own resistance or acceptance. This is, after all, why I picked up the report: to search for clues about the Indians who lived in this place, in these mountains, in this very valley, not long before us, but who've been wiped clean from the record of history, a record so recent it starts more or less with Pierce. At the start I had no interest in Pierce himself, another faceless white man, if not quite Captain Cook or Cortés, certainly not someone of interest to me. I would much rather read the journals of Indians, but they don't exist, or I should say, they don't exist in words. Pictographs in red pigment on a granite face high above Lake Chelan, directly across from where the passenger ferry docks, show human figures and animals—mountain goats, perhaps, or deer—alongside handprints and tick marks, and archaeo-logical sites show, according to carbon dating, that humans have inhabited the place for at least eight thousand years. Then there's the forest itself, with a long living history that ethnobotanists will someday parse to learn which plants were used when and how. But there are no stories in words, and since words are my currency, I sit in my hard-backed desk chair with Henry H. Pierce.

From the Okanogan, the expedition climbs a series of terraces to a high pass, and Pierce's observations grow more precise, his prose more agile and lively.

> Each terrace, free from underbrush, was in itself a
> charming picture, with its park-like area of scattered
> pines whose branches spread a grateful coolness
> athwart the trail, and cast symmetrical shadows

over the fresh, bright grass that glowed in the morning sun.

He follows this with a full paragraph on the "peculiar love-
liness of the Methow," the valley directly east of Stehekin.
If his nature-love feels slightly overwrought and dated,
his reactions to the mountains, especially, seem distinctly
familiar.

> Two grand and friendly peaks, one shaped like the
> point of an egg, the other like a pyramid—lifted their
> snow-clad summits to the clouds.... So grand and
> sudden was the vision that I named them the Wonder
> Mountains on the spot.

The description is over the top, yes, but it's unmistakably earnest, the work, I presume, of a young man, naïve
and wowed. Not unlike the new arrivals each summer in
Stehekin. Not, for that matter, unlike me when I was young.
If I'd had the power to name mountains on the day I first
spied the North Cascades, not astride a horse but behind
the wheel of a Corolla, racing through fog, when the clouds
lifted and a vast snowy jumble intruded on the winter blue,
well, I could've done worse than to choose, simply, "Wonder."

But more than majesty rings true. As the expedition
moves west, closer to Stehekin, up steep switchbacks, then
steeper ones, irritation creeps in. The mosquitoes in particular are crazy-making.

The startling whirr of the rattlesnake that accompa-
nied us along the trail had less of terror than the well-
known hum of this troublesome insect's wings, and a
camp comparatively free from the unwelcome sound
was ever after hailed with rejoicing.

Yes, yes, that's right too. I'm chuckling now as I read.
I can't count the number of days I've spent clothed neck
to toe, head net draped over a ball cap, armored against
mosquitoes or black flies. The idea of rugged explorers
"rejoicing" over a bug-free camp sounds as true as it is,
undeniably, entertaining.

The route gets rougher. Their local guide, Captain Jim
of the Chelan tribe, stops to have a few words with another
Indian, in their native tongue, about the trail ahead, and
in the morning he warns Pierce about conditions and begs
him not to be upset if one of the mules were to die that day.
They continue up, covering 1,500 vertical feet on a trail that
grows fainter by the foot with "the last 200 yards, over loose,
yielding rocks, ready to slip at the slightest pressure." When
at last they reach a high pass and get their first glimpse of
the Stehekin Valley, Pierce waxes poetic again:

As I gazed westward from a height of 6850 feet above
the sea, a scene of remarkable grandeur was presented. To the south and west were the rugged peaks
of the Cascade Mountains covered with everlasting
snow. At our feet reposed Chelan, in color like an

artificial lake of thick plate glass.... No painter could place the view on canvas and be believed.

There's no mistaking where they stand: Purple Pass. The elevation gives it away, and the view, too, which splits the space between rolling dry hills to the east and glacier-white peaks to the south and west that stagger along the lake in formation like a chess set reversed: larger peaks in front, getting smaller in the distance, shrinking toward the gold light over the Columbia. I stood there alone at twenty-two with a frame pack and pup tent, and later as I grew stronger, I returned regularly, climbing steadily, six thousand feet in seven miles, to stand there again. Every single time I've stood there I've felt moved, grateful, blessed—you could even say "pierced"—and reading the report I feel it all over again, along with unexpected affection, grudging admiration, and troubled ambivalence.

Because right then, right there, at the scene of "remarkable grandeur" while he stands in humble awe, Henry H. Pierce makes a remarkably unhumble gesture: he names a river after himself. The name won't last. The Pierce River, it turns out, has already been named the Stehekin River. (He's mistaken another tributary for the Stehekin, and the confusion allows him to confer the new name, if briefly.) And there's no reason for me to hold this against him. Naming and claiming were the practice of the day, and he was leading a federal expedition, after all. He was a white man in the right place at the right time. But I'm bothered anyway.

I'm tired of white man names, tired of white man books and white man bosses. It hasn't always been this way. I was raised to love Kit Carson and the rugged pioneers, to read little kid biographies of Nathan Hale and John Paul Jones, to read Chaucer and Shakespeare, Emerson and Thoreau, Kerouac, Snyder, Stegner, and all the rest, and by default, I grew to be an expert in and admirer of the great canon(s) of white men, who were, after all, the only ones with the license to explore or, for that matter, to write. When I began to write, I wrote like a man, and when I began to work, I worked like a man. I am not upset about any of this, exactly, but I am weary. I'm glad the river is not named Pierce. And I'm eager to read on.

They descend from Purple Pass "knee deep in dust like ashes filled with sharp fragments of rock, and constantly threatened by boulders tumbling from above." I can remember this, too, nearly giddy with recognition: that's right, that's right! The switchbacks drop most steeply at the top, where an old sheep gate stood in our time, a testament to Basque sheepherders who came after Pierce, and where the risk of rolling rocks onto hikers below runs high. In the aftermath of a large hot wildfire a decade ago, the soil has once again burned to dust-like ash, ash-like dust, which fills a boot through the seams, and from the cuff, sometimes with fragments too sharp to be "pebbles." No round word works, but "fragment" does. One long trail loop takes you twenty miles in a day, up Boulder Creek and over Purple Pass and down, and we walked this loop annually, working, clearing logs, and if there was glory in it, by the time you hit the bottom switchbacks near the lake, any glory has passed, leaving only wincing sore soles and sweat, a kind of delirious exhaustion, familiar, obviously, to Pierce.

Who, at this point, has it worse than we ever did. The men drop to the mouth of the Pierce/Stehekin only to find "a dense jungle of cottonwoods, willows, firs and underbrush . . . the matted windfall of ages, an impenetrable barrier against any approach to this head of the lake except by water." No paved road. No convenience store with ice-cream bars in a chest freezer. No cold beer in a cooler on the floorboards, left as a gift, a reward, by friends. No chainsaws, even, to clear "the matted windfall of ages." But the prose remains lively. There's a hint of Indiana Jones to it, even as irritation gives way to annoyance, as anyone who has tried to bushwhack in the North Cascades—"green hell" is the common name—can attest. "The matted windfall of ages"? How does he come up with this stuff, so spot-on, so original, while trail-beat at night in a tent in the brush?

By now, I'm convinced there must be more to the story. I dig for clues, but there's no biography with the report. A few historical articles reference the expedition, but not Pierce's backstory. One claims outright there's little known about him. I dig search engines deep to no avail. His name is not unique enough; so many other Henry Pierces. At last one lone obituary appears—from the *New York Times* no less—housed, oddly enough, among his wife's papers.

Turns out, in 1882, the summer of the expedition, Henry H. Pierce is not young at all. He's forty-eight, and he's a Civil War veteran—not unscarred, though the scars don't yet show. He joined the army as a private and worked his way to captain and before that—here comes the clincher—he was "known for translations of the Classics (Virgil, Homer, Horace) and his own compositions received marked testimonials and strong commendations from some of the most eminent scholars of the age."

Ah, so. The report is no fluke. The guy is a scholar, a linguist, who's lived a life steeped in language. Now I hear it: the rhythms of Latin under the surface, the vocabulary, the agility, the precision. At a school where I've been teaching, a translation course is required. Students who know nothing of the original languages move bland context-free definitions around like puzzle pieces to try to make meaning and music. Lately, I've been attending their post-course readings, mesmerized. Several students read translations of the same piece, and if some are dry and clunky, others are downright startling. I weep every time. Why? It's not singular genius that gets to me. I don't even think it's the mystery of language. There's something more. Usually a student or audience member fluent in (or able to stumble through) the original reads the poem aloud in Hebrew or Portuguese, Japanese or Swedish, then the students stand behind a podium to read their translations, and by the time two or three of them have hit the last line with varying emphases and wildly varied meanings, I'm floored. They're getting close, some closer than others, but they've got the same goal: to peel back words and expose the bare heart. Maybe that's why I begin to feel connected to Pierce. Not what he accomplished, not the clever turn of phrase, but the palpable desire to get it right. I've tried too, and gotten it wrong often enough. Now here he is, a voice from way back, with an unmistakable flair.

Which isn't to say I'm letting him off the hook. He's still under orders of Nelson A. Miles—the man responsible for avenging Custer's death, herding Lakota onto reservations, and chasing Chief Joseph and the Nez Perce to surrender in Canada—and William "Scorched Earth" Sherman who advocated and implemented total war against the Indians of the West. How do we reconcile that?

Pierce himself acknowledges the sheer necessity of Indian guides, not just LaFleur, but local guides with local knowledge at every step of the way, and when he describes his encounters with Indians he has the air of a benevolent slave owner or an Atticus Finch, a fair man and a gentleman. Of the ranchers in the Okanogan, for example, he says, "The tribe under Edward, their chief, are friendly and disposed to be sober and industrious." When he has a chance meeting with the well-known chief Lap-a-Loop, whose arm is in a sling from a rattlesnake bite suffered while reaping oats, Pierce is clearly impressed at the chief's toughness, how casually he shrugs it off, and he uses the opportunity to discuss philosophy with the man.

I had a long talk with Lap-a-loop concerning his plans
and hopes for life, and he expressed himself as well
pleased to till the ground in peace; indeed, evinced
an intense desire to be in all regards like his white
brother, and no longer like a "coyote."

It's easy to judge the gross condescension, but he's
obviously not Custer, not Andrew Jackson. Judged by the
standards of his time and his position, he's more than generous. Maybe, I think, it wouldn't be so bad to live beside a
river named for him after all.

Naming has been in the news here for months. The focus
is an unglamorous lake, low elevation, nearly swampy
by these cold-mountain standards, a mile from the road,
tucked in trees, and covered with lily pads. Called Coon.
Any other place the origin of that name would be obvious:
raccoons. Except that we have none. Or few. Some people
say there used to be more. Some claim "coon" was a verb, as
in people might say they'd "cooned" across a log, walking
like a raccoon. Some say an early prospector had a brother
named Coon, who may or may not be the same Charles
Edward Coon who served as lieutenant governor of Washington State from 1905 to 1909 and later as assistant secre-
tary to the U.S. Treasury, whose name is rumored to appear
in the guest book of a historic Stehekin hotel. But as of 2016,
in response to hard lobbying by activists with family ties to
the valley, the state of Washington decided once and for all

that the name referred to Wilson Howard, a black prospector, and was therefore a racist slur.

So now the lake's name is Howard.

Coon. The word itself—the "oo" as in "hoot" or "loon" or "gloom," not "noon," nothing that bright—conjures memories. Shivering in the rain watching ducks cavort on the mossy log that nearly bisects the shallow end, like a trail. The pond lilies in bloom. Sitting in snow by the shore with hot tea in a thermos cup, too scared to venture out on the frozen surface and watching flakes melt into a blue heeler's fur. Or sitting in August drinking warm beers from my pack, the warmest beers for which I've ever been thanked. Once friends visited with their kids and we went to Coon Lake. There's a single rock midlake, large enough to lounge on or leap off; it's covered in goose shit and tufts of grass, a decent short swim destination, so we swam to the rock and back to shore a few times, and we did not tell the kids there were leeches in the lake—why tell them?—but the kids discovered them anyway. "Is that a bleech?" cried the six-year-old, while his older sister dangled one impossibly long leech with glee.

What changes with the name? Howard Lake was never my favorite destination, so why do I bristle and resist, especially when doing so puts me firmly in the camp of football zealots defending a team called Redskins, a perspective I despise? On one map, the C and H converge to make Coward and maybe that's what I am, what we are, unwilling to pull ourselves from the muck of name-borne oppression. Cowards.

Maybe it's stubbornness, mundane everyday annoyance, the way you sometimes feel when a friend gets married and changes her name. (She'll return to the maiden name on Facebook, decades later, trying to reconnect.) Or maybe it's because there's some kinship, a brotherhood, a sisterhood, with everyone else who's known Coon Lake—modest, leechy, frozen and not—and the renaming somehow cleaves that bond, cedes it to more distant stakeholders, do-gooders with an agenda. Even if I share the agenda in principle, it makes me sad. I'm willing to let it go, but it makes me sad.

They say Wilson Howard lived on the shores of the lake in 1891–92, a short decade after Pierce. He sold his claims for a profit. The question that lurks is, how do we know he's black? Documents nod to one Erwin Thompson as the source, and here in town people point to locals, well-known characters, some reliable, some not so much. The last rung of skepticism, for a while, was the idea that even if it meant "black dude" maybe "coon" wasn't so bad way back then. But in legal terms, that's not how it works. The state naming board is clear on this point. We don't judge by the standards of their time but by the standards of our own. It's not their name anymore; it's ours, and "coon" nowadays is plainly a slur.

While the debate held life—"raged" was never exactly the right word—nearly everyone agreed the best solution would be to use an Indian word, but what word would that be? We have no idea. As for the Indians themselves, the naming board dutifully forwarded a copy of each of the proposals to all federally recognized tribes in the region: the Colville, Skagit, Stillaguamish, Sauk-Suiattle. No responses were received. Apparently, they didn't much care.

To be honest, I haven't cared much either. I duck controversy by nature, and in a very small community, I choose my battles wisely, and this one has seemed worth skipping. Aren't there better uses for activists' passion and bureaucrats' time? God knows there are. But sitting and reading Pierce's journals, I begin to think it would be nice to read Wilson Howard's story, to know where he came from, where he got the money to buy the claims, and where he took the money he made, how he'd describe mosquitoes or the lilies on the lake, the endless rain, the people he encountered, or the pebbles in the river. But we have nothing to go on.

We only have Pierce.

Who is, on the page, still trying to bushwhack up the valley, and at some point must pass the exact place where my cabin sits today.

> Through almost impenetrable underbrush and swampy areas, the pack train toiled and floundered, the trail growing worse and worse as the day advanced. Often, by reason of fallen logs and other obstructions, progress was alone made by taking the actual bed of the creek.

I'm admiring the words again—"toiled" and "floun-dered"—and I'm thinking of how Pierce is both on a hero's quest and likely aware of creating one. You can't translate Virgil and Homer and not know the form by rote. Mostly, I'm watching how the river widens across the road from my cabin and knowing how in August it would run too shallow to travel by boat, how even now, if not for regular mainte-nance, fallen logs obscure the land route along the banks, and vine maple bends and re-roots and tangles through the logs. If you want to get anywhere, you're in for a struggle. I'm delighted by reading Pierce's account, perversely, like watching a sibling suffer. You know how this story goes; you've been there, but this time it's not you.

When I was a kid, you could send away for a picture book that changed the setting and characters to match your little kid life: your brothers' and sisters' names, your hometown, your elementary school. Even though the type-set didn't even match—it wasn't much more than a shoddy cut-and-paste game for a high price—I wanted one desper-ately. I wonder if that's the attraction of Pierce's journals all these years later. I'm fascinated by his descriptions of familiar places, even ones that might be boring as hell to someone else, the way genealogy almost always bores any-one unrelated to the family.

The expedition, at any rate, is almost over.

At the end of twelve laborious miles, the party sets up at "an indifferent camp." (Even this phrase resonates; I've camped in less-than-ideal places, boggy or buggy, far from water or sunlight, crowded by trees or brush. Indifferent sounds about right.) They need to rest before their final ascent.

The animals are unshod and footsore, and the men are disheartened. After they've set up camp, Pierce leaves his companions and walks ahead on the trail where he runs into a miner who advises him "with great earnestness to return, saying that the ascent is impossible for packs that his best horse had tumbled from the cliffs." Historians will later make a big deal of this miner, who claimed to have lived in the area for thirty years. Thirty. Which proves Pierce wasn't the first white man to cross the mountains. Not by a long shot. Just the first to write about it. Or the first to be paid to write about it. The first to have his words preserved.

Back in camp, he finds his men in an impenetrable sleet storm—"impenetrable" has become the most repeated word in the manuscript—and eats a scanty meal of "bread and snow water." Morning brings no solace.

> Daybreak found us astir, the sleety storm still falling on the desolate scene. One of our number was sent back for a coffee pot and rations while the remainder of the party patiently expecting a breakfast, lost deferred, fostered their hopefulness by a cheerless fire.

They take a vote on whether to advance or retreat, and all but one vote for retreat. But Pierce, with Downing and LaFleur, forges on.

The sky clears and illuminates the peaks as they crest Cascade Pass, more dramatic than Purple Pass any day. But we get no descriptions of grandeur, only the relief of descending, at last, down through groves of cedars forty feet in circumference. The men must borrow a dull axe to fell a tall pine, and it takes a half day to cross a stream, but they make it down the Cascade River to the Skagit River, where they trade three horses for a canoe and float to Puget Sound. Pierce's report concludes with Sherman's endorsement, dated December 11, 1882:

> Further explorations will be made, and publication
> of the information gained should be made, as it is to
> the national interest that the timber and minerals of
> that region should be brought within the reach of the
> emigrants who will throng the Oregon and Washing-
> ton Territory as soon as the Northern Pacific Railroad
> is completed.

I'm left with the guilty pleasure of having succumbed to a predictable plot and a satisfying end.

But it's not, of course, the end.

In 1889 Alfred Downing, the illustrator, will return to Stehekin. He'll arrive during a massive wildfire that sends him out on the lake in a dory to avoid the flames, and he'll live to tell the tale. The same year, Washington Territory will achieve statehood, a development for which some recent histories give partial credit to George Washington Bush, a black pioneer whose biracial son William Owen Bush will serve in the legislature in 1890. By 1891 Stehekin will be a bustling tourist destination, attracting more people than it does today. Wilson Howard will move to the shores of Coon/Howard Lake, make a killing, and move away. By 1893 a party of thirty-five tourists, men and women both, will travel from the mouth of the river to a place just shy of Cascade Pass in seven hours thirty-five minutes. The same trip that took Pierce two treacherous days would be more or less a joyride.

And by 1883, just one year after the expedition, Henry H. Pierce will be dead.

Picture her in a desk chair under an oil lamp, inkwell beside her, an inkwell that will run dry over years—decades— while she writes the same damned letter over and over: Henry H. Pierce served honorably. I have three children, and one of them is very ill. My husband—certified here as required, married, yes, yes, never divorced—may not have died on the battlefield, but he died serving his country. Please grant me a widow's pension. Signed, dated, and notarized: Margaret Pierce. Again and again.

She's relentless. Her correspondence, housed at the Washington State Historical Society in Olympia, consists of an odd assortment of handwritten notes in the loopy script of the time and typed responses from government officials on letterhead commending her husband's service and denying benefits. Margaret Pierce is undeterred. She explains the situation: her husband had suffered from "tubercular lungs" since digging the Dutch Gap Canal on the James River in 1864, and his nervous system had been damaged by use of quinine. Now, nearly two decades later, the affliction had taken its toll.

The replies take a subtly different tack, recounting how, after his Stehekin expedition, Pierce returned to work as professor of mathematics (a translator of Homer and Virgil who also teaches math!) in West Virginia, later of military science and tactics (math *and* military tactics!) at Pacific University in Oregon, until "family afflictions" compelled him to resign and return to his regiment. He was immediately sent on a second expedition through the Cascades, perhaps in search of a better route. There he grew weak and died.

Why exactly he returned to the field is hard to figure. According to varying accounts, he was either accustomed to obeying orders or in desperate need of money. The phrase "family afflictions" suggests the latter. His son was sick; we know that much. Two years after Pierce dies, his son dies as well. (The woman sitting by the oil lamp is grieving twice over.) But "family afflictions" might be passing the buck, blaming Margaret for the army's cruel misstep in sending a sick man into the wilderness. The phrase has more than a whiff of passive aggression. For her part, Margaret Pierce insists, over and over, that her husband had been advised by doctors not to undertake work "so full of toil and exposure."

> He laid down his life that others might know . . . of the
> Okanokin and Methow. The work imposed on him,
> so peculiarly fitted for it in every other way than by
> physical strength, was more than his broken down
> body could endure, and six days march away from
> civilization he endured his last order.

In 1916 she writes again demanding a widow's pension—she is nothing if not tenacious. The response claims she's already getting twenty-five dollars a month, and twenty dollars is the most allowed a widow. In 1921 the courts find her of unsound mind, more specifically, "a lunatic," and sign over all legal authority to her daughter, Katherine. She will live as a dependent until 1939, fifty-six years longer than her husband, fifty-four years longer than her son.

She's buried with her husband, their names on the same grave marker in a Washington, D.C., cemetery. Her fate could've been due to grief or mental illness, passed down through genes, or it could've been a label convenient for those in power weary of her nagging. We'll never know. Or maybe we will. Who knows? Stories can be resurrected. Scholars do this all the time. How else does George Washington Bush, a black man, pop up on Google when you search for history of Washington State? One person carries another person to the next era, like a Sherpa or a guide, knowingly or not.

We'd know less of Henry if not for Margaret.

Sometime during all the hullabaloo around renaming Howard Lake, officials solicited for possible new names. A neighbor suggested Raven's Eye. If you hike to thirty-five hundred feet and look down on the lake, you can see the shape clearly, the beak pointing upvalley and the neck sinking into cedar grove nearly out of our sight, but the single rock, the goose poop rock we swim to, looks precisely like an eye. But it's not called Raven's Eye. It's called Howard, and I'm getting used to the change, and Pierce, by happenstance is helping. Or perhaps Margaret Pierce is. In the process of reading her letters, digressing and procrastinating, I looked up Dutch Gap Canal and stumbled on coincidence.

The digging of the Dutch Gap Canal was largely completed by black freedmen, paid African American laborers, the Twenty-Second Regiment of the Colored Infantry, a half step from slavery, a half state away. A man named Wilson Howard served in that regiment, and records show that both Howard and Pierce would've been there on August 24, 1864. Might they have met? Not likely. That would presume Pierce had been digging, and though he was not yet an officer, he was white, so he probably wasn't. The meeting is unlikely, maybe even ridiculous, but not quite preposterous. Imagine they met there, Wilson and Henry and somehow kept in touch, and after the expedition, Henry told him about this painting-perfect mountain valley, rich with opportunity, or better yet, he wrote him a letter, a letter that will someday surface. Or maybe Pierce introduced his fellow laborer to Alfred Downing who ended up returning to Stehekin the very same summer Wilson Howard arrived. Play six degrees of Kevin Bacon, and we're talking only two degrees removed, with a plausible backstory to boot. Why not?

Picture him then, a black man on a steamer or in a canoe rowing up Lake Chelan in search of fortune or adventure, escape or survival. In my imagination, because of the name, he looks like Russell Wilson, the Seahawks quarterback, young and spry, with an easy self-aware smile that says in part, I'm not what you expect. Get used to it. When I think of him this way, loosed from the controversy, loosed from history, he begins to come to life. I imagine him using his fortune to travel the world. The mining claim by the lake wouldn't be his greatest achievement, only his first. Not the end of the story, only the beginning.

Part of me still revels in Pierce. Pierce like fierce. A high, screechy sound, a hawk's cry, a fast wound, a bright morning, a not-young man with a youthful flair for words, a war survivor on the brink of a tragic end. I didn't want to like him. I like him anyway. Maybe because his words conjure a mythical unspoiled world, teetering on the brink of progress, just before the miners arrived and the settlers and road builders and orchardists. Maybe because his words remind me of my youth, of hiking with a flimsy frame pack and a secondhand tent, boots too heavy, eyes wide open to this place, every bit of it new. That's not the whole of it either. It's not newness; it's knewness. We've known the same place, Pierce and me.

Still. These days I'm less interested in what I've known than I used to be. This place may have pierced me, but it's not mine, and it's not his either, though I'm glad to have walked awhile beside him, to have made this connection, a connection that would, of course, be impossible without words. Which lands me back where I started: mourning the wordless stories, like Wilson Howard's or Margaret Pierce's or Lap-a-Loop's, the world teeming with them, like shapes on the hazy horizon you have to squint to see. If renaming makes them even a smidge more visible, even if they're partial or unfinished, based on hearsay or myth, maybe even a tad unreal, well, I have to believe that's a good thing. To make new connections, sometimes you have to immerse in the old ones, ponder and indulge. Then cleave and move on.

Last week, on a very cold day, we skied with friends toward the lake. The slog from the end of the plowed road took two long hours. A thick overnight inversion had lifted and views of the distant peaks opened and closed as swaths of storm clouds brushed across the sky. When we reached the frozen lake, the sun was not hitting it, and you cannot abide shade when you're sweaty in ten degree weather. So we backtracked to a nameless snowy knob, right at the place where the trail turns to face north, up Agnes Creek where a brine of frost coated the treetops at the elevation where the inversion had been. Now lifted, it left a clear white stripe, like the side of a chilled glass. We sat on a space blanket, so cold we had to keep gloves on while passing around crackers and cream cheese spread. We turned our faces to the sun, hoping for warmth, and Goode Ridge showed to the west, a peek-a-view clear through the tops of firs, their limbs weighty with cones, and a lone flicker worked the trunks, the busy stutter echoing in silence, and there's no reason to write this, truly, except for the hope that someday, someone will read it and think: that's right, that's right. I've been there too.

ACKNOWLEDGMENTS

Thanks to my fellow essayists—students, teachers, colleagues, and mentors—too many to name, for inspiration and camaraderie, on the page and in real life, over many years, especially Brian Doyle.

Thanks to Jill McCabe Johnson and Charles Toxey at Artsmith for the generous gift of a Madrona Residency on Orcas Island to finish these essays.

Thanks to the kind editors who have supported my work including Michelle Nijhuis, Marcus Covert, Simmons Buntin, Cara McDonald, Heidemarie Weidner, Steven Church, Dan Lehman, Joe Mackall, Joe Wilkins, Jennifer Cognard-Black, and Joyce Dyer.

Thanks to the good people at University of Washington Press including Rebecca Brinbury, Rachael Levay, Nicole Mitchell, and especially Regan Huff for her enthusiasm, feedback, and support as this project evolved, and to Susan

Marsh and Nick Neely for keen insights and helpful suggestions during review.

Much gratitude to Claire Gebben and Michele Genthon for co-steering a sinking ship with wisdom and grace and to my lifeboat buddy Sarah Van Arsdale. Here's to laughter, kindness, and survival.

Love, most of all, to my friends, neighbors, and family who live in these essays and all through them and have been kind supporters of my work over the years, especially Wendy Garfoot, Teresa Kulik, Mike Miles, Julie Higgins, Jerry Gabriel, Reneé Hudak, Shari Lehman, Terry Lavender, Mark Scherer, the Nielsens, the Barnharts, the Dickersons, Jean and Jonathan, Ron and Vicki, Tom and Maria, the Thompsons, Krautkremers, Spagnas, and Iorios. Plus the dear memory of Joon the cat. And always: Laurie.

Several of these essays were previously published, some in different form. "Slow Connection" at smokebox.net; "More Than Noise" in *From Curlers to Chainsaws: Women and Their Machines* (Michigan State University Press, 2016); "Winter Flood" at terrain.org; "Breathe" at inlandia.com; "Where You'd Rather Be" and "Post-Strayed" in *Under the Sun*; "How to Brine an Elk Steak" in *Portland*; "When We Talk about Courage" in *Cirque*; "So Many Rings" in the *Normal School*; "Together We Pause," "The Injured Bear," "Away from Shore," and "The Tree in the River" in *High Country News*; "The Fiddler on the Rock" in *Fort Collins Magazine*;

"Here in the WUI" in *Sierra*; "Fire One, Fire Two" in *River Teeth*; "Confessional Roots" in *Hotel Amerika*; "Pierce" in *High Desert Journal*.